WAITIN[...]

ENDGAME, &
OTHER PLAYS

by
Jeffery Fisher, M.F.A.   *and*   *James L. Roberts, Ph.D.*
University of Tennessee   *Department of English*
                            University of Nebraska

Editor
Gary Carey, M.A.
University of Colorado

INCORPORATED
LINCOLN, NEBRASKA 68501

ISBN 0-8220-1354-1

CONTENTS

BECKETT NOTES

BRIEF LIFE OF SAMUEL BECKETT

Samuel Beckett was born in Dublin, Ireland, in 1906, the second
son of comfortable middle-class parents who were a part of the
Protestant minority in a predominantly Catholic society. He was
provided with an excellent education, graduating from Trinity Col-
lege, Dublin, with a major emphasis in French and Italian. His first
job was as a teacher of English in the Ecole Normale Supérieure in
Paris. In 1931, he returned to Ireland as a lecturer in French literature, and he received his masters degree in French from Dublin and
subsequently returned to Paris as a teacher in 1932. He has made
Paris his home since that time, except for visits abroad and a retreat
to the Unoccupied Zone in Vichy, France, during 1942-44.

Beckett found teaching uncongenial to his creative activities and
soon turned all of his attention to writing. During the 1930s and
'40s, his writing consisted of critical studies (Proust and others),
poems, and two novels (*Murphy* and *Watt*), all written in English.
In the late 1940s, he changed from writing in English to writing in
French. Part of the reason for this was his basic rejection of Ireland
as his homeland. When asked why he found Ireland uncongenial, he
offered the same explanation that has been given by other famous
Irish expatriates, such as Sean O'Casey and James Joyce. He could
not tolerate the strict censorship of so many aspects of life, especially the arbitrary censoring of many works of literature by the
Catholic clergy. In addition, the political situation created an op-
pressive anti-intellectualism. Even after he became famous, he refused to allow some of his plays to be presented in Ireland. In 1958,
during the International Theater Festival in Dublin, a play of his
compatriot O'Casey was banned, and Beckett, in protest, withdrew
his plays, which have not been seen in Ireland since then.

Since the major portion of his dramas were composed in French
and first presented in Paris, many critics find difficulty in classify-
ing Beckett's works: should he be considered a French or an Irish

writer? The nature of his characters, even when named Vladimir and Estragon, seems to be more characteristically Irish than any other nationality. Essentially, it should be a moot question because Beckett, when composing in French, was his own translator into English and vice versa. Thus his works do not suffer from another translator's tampering with them, and his great plays now belong to the realm of world literature.

SAMUEL BECKETT AND THE THEATER OF THE ABSURD

With the appearance of *En Attendant Godot* (*Waiting for Godot*) at the Théâtre de Babylone in Paris in 1953, the literary world was shocked by the appearance of a drama so different and yet so intriguing that it virtually created the term "Theater of the Absurd," and the entire group of dramas which developed out of this type of theater is always associated with the name of Samuel Beckett. His contribution to this particular genre allows us to refer to him as the grand master, or father, of the genre. While other dramatists have also contributed significantly to this genre, Beckett remains its single, most towering figure.

This movement known as the Theater of the Absurd was not a consciously conceived movement, and it has never had any clear-cut philosophical doctrines, no organized attempt to win converts, and no meetings. Each of the main playwrights of the movement seem to have developed independently of each other. The playwrights most often associated with the movement are Samuel Beckett, Eugene Ionesco, Jean Genet, and Arthur Adamov. The early plays of Edward Albee and Harold Pinter fit into this classification, but these dramatists have also written plays that move far away from the Theater of the Absurd's basic elements.

In viewing the plays that comprise this movement, we must forsake the theater of coherently developed situations, we must forsake characterizations that are rooted in the logic of motivation and reaction, we must sometimes forget settings that bear an intrinsic realistic, or obvious relationship to the drama as a whole, we must forget the use of language as a tool of logical communication, and we must forget cause-and-effect relationships found in traditional ramas. By their use of a number of puzzling devices, these play-rights have gradually accustomed audiences to a new kind of rela-onship between theme and presentation. In these seemingly queer nd fantastic plays, the external world is often depicted as menac-g, devouring, and unknown; the settings and situations often ake us vaguely uncomfortable; the world itself seems incoherent nd frightening and strange, but at the same time, it seems haunt-gly poetic and familiar.

These are some of the reasons which prompt the critic to classify nem under the heading "Theater of the Absurd"—a title which omes not from a dictionary definition of the word "absurd," but ther from Martin Esslin's book *The Theatre of the Absurd*, in hich he maintains that these dramatists write from a "sense of etaphysical anguish at the absurdity of the human condition." ut other writers such as Kafka, Camus, and Sartre have also gued from the same philosophical position. The essential differ-ce is that critics like Camus have presented their arguments in a ghly formal discourse with logical and precise views which prove eir theses within the framework of traditional forms. On the con-ary, the Theater of the Absurd seeks to wed form and content into a indissoluble whole in order to gain a further unity of meaning d impact. This theater, as Esslin has pointed out, "has renounced guing *about* the absurdity of the human condition; it merely esents it in being—that is, in terms of concrete stage images of the surdity of existence."

Too often, however, the viewer notes only these basic similarities d fails to note the distinctive differences in each dramatist. Since ese writers do not belong to any deliberate or conscious move-ent, they should be evaluated for their individual concerns, as well for their contributions to the total concept of the Theater of the surd. In fact, most of these playwrights consider themselves to be nely rebels and outsiders, isolated in their own private worlds. As ted above, there have been no manifestoes, no theses, no confer-ces, and no collaborations. Each has developed along his own ique lines; each in his own way is individually and distinctly dif-ent. Therefore, it is important to see how Beckett both belongs to e Theater of the Absurd and, equally important, how he differs m the other writers associated with this movement. First, let us te a few of the basic differences.

Differences

One of Samuel Beckett's main concerns is the polarity of existence. In *Waiting for Godot, Endgame,* and *Krapp's Last Tape,* we
have such characteristic polarities as sight versus blindness, life—
death, time present—time past, body—intellect, waiting—not waiting, going—not going, and dozens more. One of Beckett's main concerns, then, seems to be characterizing man's existence in terms of
these polarities. To do this, Beckett groups his characters in pairs;
for example, we have Vladimir and Estragon, or Didi and Gogo,
Hamm and Clov, Pozzo and Lucky, Nagg and Nell, and Krapp's
present voice and past voice. Essentially, however, Beckett's characters remain a puzzle which each individual viewer must solve.

In contrast to Beckett, Eugene Ionesco's characters are seen in
terms of singularity. Whereas Beckett's characters stand in pairs
outside of society, but converse with each other, Ionesco's characters are placed in the midst of society—but they stand alone in an
alien world with no personal identity and no one with whom they
can communicate. For example, the characters in *The Bald Soprano*
are *in* society, but they scream meaningless phrases at each other,
and there is no communication. And whereas Beckett's plays take
place on strange and alien landscapes (some of the settings of his
plays remind one of a world transformed by some holocaust or
created by some surrealist), Ionesco's plays are set against the most
traditional elements in our society—the standard English drawing
room in *The Bald Soprano,* a typical street scene in *Rhinoceros,*
and an average academic study in *The Lesson,* etc.

The language of the two playwrights also differs greatly. Beckett's dialogue recalls the disjointed phantasmagoria of a dream
world; Ionesco's language is rooted in the banalities, cliches, and
platitudes of everyday speech; Beckett uses language to show man
isolated in the world and unable to communicate because language
is a barrier to communication. Ionesco, on the other hand, uses language to show the failure of communication because there is nothing to say; in *The Bald Soprano,* and other plays, the dialogue is
filled with cliches and platitudes.

In contrast to the basic sympathy we feel for both Beckett's and
Ionesco's characters, Jean Genet's characters almost revile the audience from the moment that they appear on the stage. His theme is
stated more openly. He is concerned with the hatred which exists in
the world. In *The Maids,* for example, each maid hates not just her

employer and not just her own sister, but also her own self. Therefore, she plays the other roles so as to exhaust her own hatred of
herself against herself. Basically, then, there is a great sense of re-
pugnance in Genet's characters. This revulsion derives partially
from the fact that Genet's dramatic interest, so different from Beckett's and Ionesco's, is in the psychological exploration of man's
predilection to being trapped in his own egocentric world, rather
than facing the realities of existence. Man, for Genet, is trapped by
his own fantastic illusions; man's absurdity results partially from
the fact that he prefers his own disjointed images to those of reality.
In Genet's directions for the production of *The Blacks,* he writes
that the play should never be played before a totally black audience. If there are no white people present, then one of the blacks in
the audience must wear a white mask; if the black refuses, then a
white mannequin must be used, and the actors must play the drama
for this mannequin. There must at least be a symbol of a white
audience, someone for the black actors to revile.

In contrast to Beckett, Arthur Adamov, in his themes, is more
closely aligned to the Kafkaesque, existentialistic school, but his
technique is that of the Theater of the Absurd. His interest is in establishing some proof that the individual does exist, and he shows
how man becomes more alienated from his fellow man as he attempts to establish his own personal identity. For example, in *Professor Taranne,* the central character, hoping to prove his innocence
of a certain accusation, actually convicts himself through his own
defense. For Adamov, man attempting to prove his own existence
actually proves, ironically, that he does not exist. Therefore language, for Adamov, serves as an inadequate system of communication and, actually, in some cases serves to the detriment of man,
since by language and man's use of language, man often finds himself trapped in the very circumstances he previously hoped to avoid.
Ultimately, Adamov's characters fail to communicate because each
is interested only in his own egocentric self. Each character pro-
pounds his own troubles and his own achievements, but the words
reverberate, as against a stone wall. They are heard only by the
audience. Adamov's plays are often grounded in a dream-world atmosphere, and while they are presenting a series of outwardly confusing scenes of almost hallucinative quality, they, at the same time,
attack or denounce the confusion present in modern man.

Characteristic of all these writers is a notable absence of any ex-

cess concern with sex. Edward Albee, an American, differs signifi
cantly in his emphasis and concern with the sexual substructure c
society. The overtones of homosexuality in *The Zoo Story* are ca
ried further until the young man in *The American Dream* become
the physical incarnation of a muscular and ideally handsome, youn
sexual specimen who, since he has no inner feelings, passively allow
anyone "to take pleasure from my groin." In *The Sandbox,* th
angel of death is again seen as the musclebound young sexual spec
men who spends his time scantily dressed and performing calisther
ics on a beach while preparing for a career in Hollywood.

Similarities

Since all of the writers have varying concerns, they also hav
much in common because their works reflect a moral and philc
sophical climate in which most of our civilization finds itself toda
Again, as noted above, even though there are no manifestoes, no
any organized movements, there are still certain concerns that ar
basic to all of the writers, and Beckett's works are concerned wit
these basic ideas.

Beyond the technical and strange illusionary techniques whic
prompt the critic to group these plays into a category, there ar
larger and, ultimately, more significant concerns by which eac
dramatist, in spite of his artistic differences, is akin to the other
Aside from such similarities as violation of traditional beginnin
middle, and end structure (exposition, complication, and denoue
ment) or the refusal to tell a straightforward, connected story wit
a proper plot, or the disappearance of traditional dramatic form
and techniques, these dramatists are all concerned with the failur
of communication in modern society which leaves man alienatec
moreover, they are all concerned with the lack of individuality an
the overemphasis on conformity in our society, and they use th
dramatic elements of time and place to imply important ideas
finally, they reject traditional logic for a type of non-logic which u
timately implies something about the nature of the univers
Implicit in many of these concerns is an attack on a society or
world which possesses no set standards of values or behavior.

Foremost, all of these dramatists of the absurd are concerne
with the lack of communication. In Edward Albee's plays, eac
character is existing within the bounds of his own private ego. Eac
makes a futile attempt to get another character to understand hin

but as the attempt is heightened, there is more alienation. Thus, finally, because of a lack of communication, Peter, the conformist in *The Zoo Story,* is provoked into killing Jerry, the individualist; and in *The Sandbox,* a continuation of *The American Dream,* Mommy and Daddy bury Grandma because she talks incessantly but says nothing significant. The irony is that Grandma is the only character who does say anything significant, but Mommy and Daddy, the people who discard her, are incapable of understanding her.

In Ionesco's plays, this failure of communication often leads to even more drastic results. Akin to the violence in Albee's *Zoo Story,* the professor in *The Lesson* must kill his student partly because she doesn't understand his communication. Berenger, in *The Killers,* has uttered so many cliches that by the end of the play, he has convinced even himself that the killers should kill him. In *The Chairs,* the old people, needing to express their thoughts, address themselves to a mass of empty chairs which, as the play progresses, crowd all else off the stage. In *Maid to Marry,* communication is so bad that the maid, when she appears on the stage, turns out to be a rather homely man. And ultimately in *Rhinoceros,* the inability to communicate causes an entire race of so-called rational human beings to be metamorphosed into a herd of rhinoceroses, thereby abandoning all hopes of language as a means of communication.

In Adamov's *Professor Taranne,* the professor, in spite of all his desperate attempts, is unable to get people to acknowledge his identity because there is no communication. Likewise, Pinter's plays show individuals grouped on the stage, but each person fails to achieve any degree of effective communication. This concern with communication is finally carried to its illogical extreme in two works: in Genet's *The Blacks,* one character says, "We shall even have the decency—a decency learned from you—to make communication impossible." And in another, Beckett's *Act Without Words I,* we have our first play in this movement that uses absolutely no dialogue. And even without dialogue, all the action on the stage suggests the inability of man to communicate.

Beckett's characters are tied together by a fear of being left entirely alone, and they therefore cling to one last hope of establishing some kind of communication. His plays give the impression that man is totally lost in a disintegrating society, or, as in *Endgame,* that man is left alone after society has disintegrated. In *Waiting for Godot,* two derelicts are seen conversing in a repetitive, strangely

fragmented dialogue that possesses an illusory, haunting effec
while they are waiting for Godot, a vague, never-defined being wh
will bring them some communication about—what? Salvation
Death? An impetus for living? A reason for dying? No one knows
and the safest thing to say is that the two are probably waiting fc
someone or something which will give them an impetus to continu
living or, at least, something which will give meaning and directio
to their lives. As Beckett clearly demonstrates, those who rus
hither and yon in search of meaning find it no quicker than thos
who sit and wait. The "meaning" about life that these tramps hop
for is never stated precisely. But Beckett never meant his play to b
a "message play," in which one character would deliver
"message." The message here is conveyed through the interaction c
the characters and primarily through the interaction of the tw
tramps. Everyone leaves the theater with the knowledge that thes
tramps are strangely tied to one another; even though they bicke
and fight, and even though they have exhausted all conversation–
notice that the second act is repetitive and almost identical—th
loneliness and weakness in each calls out to the other, and they ar
held by a mystical bond of interdependence. In spite of this strang
dependency, however, neither is able to communicate with th
other. The other two characters, Pozzo and Lucky, are on a journe
without any apparent goal and are symbolically tied together. On
talks, the other says nothing. The waiting of Vladimir and Estrago
and the journeying of Pozzo and Lucky offer themselves as cor
trasts of various activities in the modern world—all of which lead t
no fruitful end; therefore, each pair is hopelessly alienated from th
other pair. For example, when Pozzo falls and yells for help, Vlad
mir and Estragon continue talking, although nothing is commun
cated in their dialogue; all is hopeless, or as Vladimir aphoristicall
replies to one of Estragon's long discourses, "We are all born mac
Some remain so." In their attempts at conversation and commun
cation, these two tramps have a fastidious correctness and a grav
propriety that suggest that they could be socially accepted; bt
their fastidiousness and propriety are inordinately comic when cor
trasted with their ragged appearance.

Their fumbling ineffectuality in their attempts at conversatio
seems to represent the ineptness of all mankind in its attempt ⟨
communication. And it rapidly becomes apparent that Vladim
and Estragon, as representatives of modern man, cannot formula⟨

any cogent or useful resolution or action; and what is more pathetic, they cannot communicate their helpless longings to one another. While failing to possess enough individualism to go their separate ways, they nevertheless are different enough to embrace most of our society. In the final analysis, their one positive gesture is their strength to wait. But man is, ultimately, terribly alone in his waiting. Ionesco shows the same idea at the end of *Rhinoceros* when we see Berenger totally alone as a result, partly, of a failure in communication.

Each dramatist, therefore, presents a critique of modern society by showing the total collapse of communication. The technique used is that of evolving a theme about communication by presenting a series of seemingly disjointed speeches. The accumulative effect of these speeches is a devastating commentary on the failure of communication in modern society.

In conjunction with the general attack on communication, the second aspect common to these dramatists is the lack of individuality encountered in modern civilization. Generally, the point seems to be that man does not know himself. He has lost all sense of individualism and either functions isolated and alienated, or else finds himself lost amid repetition and conformity.

Jean Genet's play *The Maids* opens with the maid Claire playing the role of her employer while her sister Solange plays the role of Claire. Therefore, we have Claire referring to Solange as Claire. By the time the audience realizes that the two sisters are imitating someone else, each character has lost her individualism; therefore, when Claire later portrays Solange, who portrays the employer, and vice versa, we gradually realize that part of Genet's intent is to illustrate the total lack of individuality and, furthermore, to show that each character becomes vibrantly alive only when functioning in the image of another personality.

Other dramatists present their attack on society's destruction of individualism by different means, but the attack still has the same thematic intent. In Albee's *The American Dream,* Mommy and Daddy are obviously generic names for any mommy and daddy. Albee is not concerned with individualizing his characters. They remain types and, as types, are seen at times in terms of extreme burlesque. So, unlike Beckett's tramps, and more like Ionesco's characters, Albee's people are seen as Babbitt-like caricatures and satires on the "American Dream" type; the characters remain mannequins

with no delineations. Likewise in Ionesco's *The Bald Soprano,* the
Martins assume the roles of the Smiths and begin the play over because there is no distinction between the two sets of characters.

Perhaps more than any of the other dramatists of the absurd, Ionesco has concerned himself almost exclusively with the failure of
individualism, especially in his most famous play, *Rhinoceros.* To
repeat, in this play, our society today has emphasized conformity to
such an extent and has rejected individualism so completely that
Ionesco demonstrates with inverse logic how stupid it is *not* to conform with all society and be metamorphosed into a rhinoceros. This
play aptly illustrates how two concerns of the absurdists—lack of
communication and the lack of individualism—are combined, each
to support the other. Much of Ionesco's dialogue in this play seems
to be the distilled essence of the commonplace. One cliche follows
another, and yet, in contrast, this dialogue is spoken within the
framework of a wildly improbable situation. In a typically common
street scene, with typically common cliches about weather and work
being uttered, the morning calm is shattered by a rhinoceros charg-
ing through the streets. Then two rhinoceroses, then more. Ridiculous arguments then develop as to whether they are African or Asi-
atic rhinoceroses. We soon learn that there is an epidemic of meta-
morphoses; everyone is changing into rhinoceroses. Soon only three
individuals are left. Then in the face of this absurd situation, we
have the equally appalling justifications and reasons in favor of
being metamorphosed advocated in such cliches as "We must join
the crowd," "We must move with the times," and "We've got to
build our life on new foundations," etc. Suddenly it seems almost
foolish *not* to become a rhinoceros. In the end, Berenger's sweet-
heart, Daisy, succumbs to the pressures of society, relinquishes her
individualism, and joins the society of rhinoceroses—not because
she wants to, but rather because she is afraid not to. She cannot revolt against society and remain a human being. Berenger is left
alone, totally isolated with his individualism. And what good is his
humanity in a world of rhinoceroses?

At first glance, it would seem obvious that Ionesco wishes to indicate the triumph of the individual, who, although caught in a society that has gone mad, refuses to surrender his sense of identity.
But if we look more closely, we see that Ionesco has no intention of
leaving us on this hopeful and comforting note.

In his last speech, Berenger makes it clear that his stand is rer dered absurd. What does his humanity avail him in a world of beasts? Finally, he wishes that he also had changed; now it is too late. All he can do is feebly reassert his joy in being human. His statement carries little conviction. This is how Ionesco deals with the haunting theme of the basic meaning and value of personal identity in relationship to society. If one depends *entirely* upon the society in which one lives for a sense of reality and identity, it is impossible to take a stand against that society without reducing oneself to nothingness in the process. Berenger instinctively felt repelled by the tyranny that had sprung up around him, but he had no sense of identity that would have enabled him to combat this evil with anything resembling a positive force. Probably any action he could have taken would have led to eventual defeat, but defeat would have been infinitely preferable to the limbo in which he is finally consigned. Ionesco has masterfully joined two themes: the lack of individualism and the failure of communication. But unlike Beckett, who handles the same themes by presenting his characters as derelicts and outcasts from society, Ionesco's treatment seems even more devastating because he places them in the very middle of the society from which they are estranged.

Ultimately, the absurdity of man's condition is partially a result of his being compelled to exist without his individualism in a society which does not possess any degree of effective communication. Essentially, therefore, the Theater of the Absurd is not a positive drama. It does not try to prove that man can exist in a meaningless world, as did Camus and Sartre, nor does it offer any solution; instead, it demonstrates the absurdity and illogicality of the world we live in. Nothing is ever settled; there are no positive statements; no conclusions are ever reached, and what few actions there are have no meaning, particularly in relation to the action. That is, one action carries no more significance than does its opposite action. For example, the man's tying his shoe in *The Bald Soprano*—a common occurrence—is magnified into a momentous act, while the appearance of rhinoceroses in the middle of a calm afternoon seems to be not at all consequential and evokes only the most trite and insignificant remarks. Also, Pozzo and Lucky's frantic running and searching are no more important than Vladimir and Estragon's sitting and waiting. And Genet presents his blacks as outcasts and misfits from society, but refrains from making any positive statement regarding the black person's role in our society. The question of whether soci-

ety is to be integrated or segregated is, to Genet, a matter of abso-
lute indifference. It would still be society, and the individual would
still be outside it.

No conclusions or resolutions can ever by offered, therefore, because these plays are essentially circular and repetitive in nature
The Bald Soprano begins over again with a new set of characters
and other plays end at the same point at which they began, thus ob-
viating any possible conclusions or positive statements. *The American Dream* ends with the coming of a second child, this time one
who is fully grown and the twin to the other child who had years
before entered the family as a baby and upset the static condition
thematically, the play ends as it began. In all of these playwrights
dramas, the sense of repetition, the circular structure, the static
quality, the lack of cause and effect, and the lack of apparent pro
gression all suggest the sterility and lack of values in the modern
world.

Early critics referred to the Theater of the Absurd as a theater in
transition, meaning that it was to lead to something different. So
far this has not happened, but the Theater of the Absurd is rapidly
becoming accepted as a distinct genre in its own right. The themes
utilized by the dramatists of this movement are not new; thus, the
success of the plays must often depend upon the effectiveness of the
techniques and the new ways by which the dramatists illustrate
their themes. The techniques are still so new, however, that many
people are confused by a production of one of these plays. Yet if the
technique serves to emphasize the absurdity of man's position in the
universe, then to present this concept by a series of ridiculous situa
tions is only to render man's position even more absurd; and in ac
tuality, the techniques then reinforce that very condition which the
dramatists bewail. In other words, to present the failure of com
munication by a series of disjointed and seemingly incoherent utter
ances lends itself to the accusation that functionalism is carried to
ridiculous extreme. But this is exactly what the absurdist wants t
do. He is tired of logical discourses pointing out step-by-step the ab
surdity of the universe: he begins with the philosophical premise
that the universe is absurd, and then creates plays which illustrat
conclusively that the universe is indeed absurd and that perhap
this play is another additional absurdity.

In conclusion, if the public can accept these unusual uses of tech
nique to support thematic concerns, then we have plays which

dramatically present powerful and vivid views on the absurdity of the human condition—an absurdity which is the result of the destruction of individualism and the failure of communication, of man's being forced to conform to a world of mediocrity where no action is meaningful. As the tragic outcasts of these plays are presented in terms of burlesque, man is reminded that his position and that of human existence in general is essentially absurd. Every play in the Theater of the Absurd movement mirrors the chaos and basic disorientation of modern man. Each play laughs in anguish at the confusion that exists in contemporary society; hence, all share a basic point of view, while varying widely in scope and structure.

Waiting for Godot

LIST OF CHARACTERS

Vladimir (Didi)
An old derelict dressed like a tramp; along with his companion of many years, he comes to a bleak, desolate place to wait for Godot.

Estragon (Gogo)
Vladimir's companion of many years who is overly concerned with his physical needs, but is repeatedly told by Vladimir that, above all, they must wait for Godot.

Pozzo
A traveling man dressed rather elaborately; he arrives driving another man (Lucky) forward by means of a rope around the latter's neck.

Lucky
The "slave" who obeys Pozzo absolutely.

Boy Messenger I and Boy Messenger II
Each is a young boy who works for "Mr. Godot" and brings Vladimir and Estragon news about "Mr. Godot"; apparently he takes

messages back to "Mr. Godot."

Godot
He never appears in the drama, but he is an entity that Vladimir and Estragon are waiting for.

DRAMATIC DIVISIONS
Even though the drama is divided into two acts, there are other natural divisions. For the sake of discussion, the following, rather obvious, scene divisions will be referred to:

ACT I: (1) Vladimir and Estragon Alone
   (2) Arrival of Pozzo and Lucky: Lucky's Speech
   (3) Departure of Pozzo and Lucky: Vladimir and Estragon Alone
   (4) Arrival of Boy Messenger
   (5) Departure of Boy Messenger: Vladimir and Estragon Alone

ACT II: (1) Vladimir and Estragon Alone
   (2) Arrival of Pozzo and Lucky
   (3) Departure of Pozzo and Lucky: Vladimir and Estragon Alone
   (4) Arrival of Boy Messenger
   (5) Departure of Boy Messenger: Vladimir and Estragon Alone

The above divisions of the play are Beckett's way of making a statement about the nature of the play—that is, the play is circular in structure, and a third act (or even a fourth or fifth act, etc.) could be added, having the exact same structure. For further discussion, see the section on Circular Structure.

CRITICAL ANALYSIS

ACT I: VLADIMIR AND ESTRAGON

The rising curtain exposes a landscape that is strange and alien. It most resembles some strange place in outer space with its haunting and brooding sense of despair. A country road or an actual lonely road is the main setting, and there is a single tree. We know there is a ditch on the other side of the road because immediately Estragon tells Vladimir that he slept last night in the ditch. The loneliness and the isolation of the setting sets the tone for the play. The idea of a road implies a journey, a movement, a purpose to life, but we see, instead, two deserted, isolated figures with no place to go and with no journey to look forward to. These figures are dressed in rags and tatters, clothes that would be worn by two tramps in an old, second-rate burlesque production. Thus the setting and the clothing make an ominous comment before we are too far into the drama.

The play opens with Estragon involved in a tremendous struggle —but not a struggle of a highly metaphysical nature; instead, it is a physical struggle to get his stuck boot off his sore foot. The struggle has literally exhausted him, and he gives up the struggle with the opening words of the play: *"Nothing to be done"* (emphasis ours). Estragon's words are repeated two more times by Vladimir in the next moments of the play, and variations of this phrase become one of the central statements of the drama. The phrase is innocent enough in itself and obviously directed toward a specific struggle— the removal of the boot. But as frustrating as the boot is, this is still a minor concern when compared to what Estragon and Vladimir are to do with the problem of waiting for Godot. In response to Estragon's struggle with his foot, Vladimir ignores the immediate physical problem but agrees with Estragon metaphysically that there is "nothing to be done," even though he has not "yet tried everything."

Thus the two opening speeches, innocent and simple enough in themselves, set the tone for the entire drama. The words carry a foreboding overtone which will be later associated with the word "appalled," or as Vladimir calls it, "AP-PALLED," and also the two tramps' inability to laugh.

After the opening words, we find that the two tramps are linked to each other in some undefined, ambiguous way. Vladimir greets Estragon with the comment "I thought you were gone forever," and since they are "together again at last," they will "have to celebrate." Vladimir then discovers that Estragon spent the night "in a ditch . . . over there" and that he was beaten by "the same lot as usual." This reference to a beaten man in a ditch carries overtones of other matters, but cannot be definitely correlated. For example, this could be an oblique reference to the biblical story of the Good Samaritan who finds a man beaten, robbed, and thrown into a ditch and rescues him. But no Good Samaritan has come to Estragon's rescue. Instead, he has apparently spent the entire night alone in the ditch, which means that both of them are, as their clothes indicate, in the most extreme, impoverished condition that they have ever known.

Estragon remains concerned with his boots; Vladimir, however, is extremely impatient and finds the conversation about the boots to be profitless. He turns the conversation to more abstract matters. Very early in the play, then, the difference between the two tramps is established: Estragon is concerned about immediate, practical problems—the removal of his boots, the beating, and now his aching foot; Vladimir, in contrast, laments the general nature of their sufferings by remembering better days that used to be. Whereas Estragon's foot *hurts*, Vladimir is concerned with suffering of a different nature.

The philosophical concept of the nature of suffering is first introduced here by the contrasting physical ailments of each character: Estragon has sore feet which *hurt* him, and Vladimir has some type of painful urinary infection which causes him to suffer; one character *hurts* and the other one *suffers*. Ultimately, the physical disabilities characterize the two men (an aching foot is easier to locate and describe than is a painful urinary infection) and also symbolize the various spiritual disabilities of the two characters.

Vladimir's thoughts shift from his urinary problems to the biblical concept of "Hope deferred maketh the something sick . . ." but he is unable to complete the proverb. (See *Proverbs* 13:12: "Hope deferred maketh the heart sick, but a desire fulfilled is a tree of life.") The proverb fits Vladimir and Estragon's condition perfectly since we will see them in a state of sickness of heart; their hopes are constantly deferred as they continually wait for Godot, and their desires are never fulfilled since Godot never arrives. Vladimir then concludes as did Estragon: "Nothing to be done."

Estragon has not gotten his boot off, and he looks inside it to see what was causing the difficulty. Vladimir then chastises Estragon for one of man's most common faults: blaming one's boots for the faults of one's foot. This accusation, of course, refers to the tendency of all of mankind to blame any external thing—boots, society, ircumstances, etc.—for deficiencies in one's own nature. It is easier or Estragon to blame the boots for his aching feet than to blame his wn feet.

The idea of Estragon's foot hurting and Vladimir's suffering, ombined with their appalling human condition, causes Vladimir to ealize again that there is "nothing to be done." This suffering and ack of hope turn Vladimir's thoughts to the suffering of the two hieves on the cross and their lack of hope. Then from the Old Testament proverb about hope, Vladimir's thoughts turn to the New 'estament and the possibility of hope expressed in the story of Christ and the two thieves on the cross. There were *two* thieves, as here are now *two* tramps, and *one* of the thieves was saved; therefore, maybe there may be hope for either Vladimir or Estragon if hey repent—but there is nothing to repent of, except being born. This remark causes "Vladimir to break into a hearty laugh which he immediately stifles," and he reminds Estragon that "one daren't ven laugh any more"; one may "merely smile." This comment is another early indication of the seriousness of their condition. Vladinir's apprehension over laughing suggests that they both have a nagging awareness of the precariousness and insecurity of their condition, a condition that extends beyond their physical concerns.

In the discussion of the thieves, Estragon is unable to participate ully because he can't remember the details. In frustration, Vladimir ells to Estragon: "Come on . . . return the ball can't you, once in a vay?" Vladimir's complaint is descriptive of much of the dialogue in he remainder of the play; it is very much like two people playing a game with one another and one is unable to keep the ball in play. Estragon constantly fails to "keep the ball in play"; that is, hroughout the drama, he is unable to sustain his end of the conversation. Even in response to the matter of being saved "from hell" or 'from death," Estragon merely replies, "Well what of it?" Therefore, even if they were to repent, Estragon can't understand what hey might be saved from, who their savior would be, and, furthermore, why the four Gospels differ so significantly. The discussion is brought firmly to a close with Estragon's pronouncement: "People are bloody ignorant apes."

From this discussion, the two tramps confront the central problem of the play. Estragon looks about the bleak, desolate landscape and tells Vladimir: "Let's go." The recurring thematic refrain is hen put forth: they can't leave because they are "waiting for

Godot." They are not sure they are in the right place; they are not sure they are here on the correct day; they are not sure what day of the week it is (maybe it is yesterday); they think they were to meet Godot on Saturday, but if today is Saturday, is it the right Saturday? At least, they are fairly certain that they were to meet by a tree, and there is only one tree on the horizon, but it could be either a bush or a dead tree. The tree, whatever its symbolic value (the cross, the hanging tree, spring's renewal), is a rather pathetic specimen and cannot be a very hopeful sign. Completely frustrated, they resign themselves to waiting. Vladimir paces, and Estragon sleeps.

Suddenly, Vladimir, feeling lonely, awakens Estragon, who awakens from his dream with a start. Estragon wants to tell about his dream (or nightmare), but Vladimir refuses to listen to it. Estragon's nightmare, even without its subject being revealed, symbolizes the various fears that these tramps feel in this alienated world. Vladimir's refusal to listen suggests his fear and apprehension of all of life and of certain things that are best left unsaid. Estragon, then, unable to tell about his nightmare, tries to tell a joke about an Englishman in a brothel. Again Vladimir refuses to listen and walks off.

Estragon's attempt to tell his nightmare and then his attempt to tell the joke about the Englishman—a story that is never finished— represent an effort to pass the time while the two are waiting for Godot. Since they have been waiting and will be waiting for an indeterminate time, the essential problem is what to do with one's life while waiting, how to pass the time while waiting.

When Vladimir returns, the two embrace and then they try to decide what they are going to do while waiting. During the embrace, the tender, fraternal rapport of the moment is suddenly broken by Estragon's mundane observation that Vladimir smells of garlic. This technique is typical of Beckett's method of deflating man's pretensions by allowing the absurd and the vulgar to dominate the action.

The eternal question returns: what to do while waiting? Estragon suggests that perhaps they could hang themselves. That would certainly put an end to their waiting. Hanging also has another incentive: it would excite them sexually and cause each to have an erection and an ejaculation. But the matter of hanging creates some problems. Vladimir should hang himself first because he is the heaviest. If the straggly tree does not break under Vladimir's heavier weight, then it would be strong enough for Estragon's lighter weight. But if Estragon went first, the tree might break when Vladimir tried it, and then Estragon (Gogo) would be dead, and poor Vladimir (Didi) would be alive and completely alone. These considerations are simply too weighty to solve. Man's attempts to solve things rationally bring about all types of difficulties; it is best to do nothing—"It's safer." Accordingly, they decide to "wait and see what [Godot] says," hoping that he, or someone, will make a decision about them or that something will be done for them. They will make no effort to change their rather intolerable and impossible situation, but, instead, they will hope that someone or some objective event will eventually change things for them.

Having resolved to wait for Godot, they then wonder what he might offer them and, even more important, "what exactly did we ask him for?" Whatever it was they asked him for, Godot was equally vague and equivocal in his reply. Maybe he is at home thinking it over, consulting friends, correspondents, banks, etc. The tramps' entire discussion about Godot indicates how little, if indeed anything at all, they know of this Godot. The fact that Vladimir can't remember what they asked of Godot indicates that they are unable to understand their own needs. They rely on someone else to tell them what they need. Similarly, the request and the possible response are discussed in terms of a person requesting a bank loan or some type of financial transaction. A philosophical question then begins to emerge: how does one relate to Godot? If he is God, can one enter into a business contract with this person? And if so, where is He? If Godot (or God) has to consult many outside sources before replying or appearing, then Vladimir and Estragon's condition is not very reassuring. And, if, as it now begins to become obvious, Vladimir and Estragon represent modern man in his relationship with God (Godot), then the modern condition of man is disturbingly precarious.

What, then, is man in this modern world? He is a beggar or a tramp reduced to the most dire circumstances: he is lost, not knowing where to turn. He is denied all rights, even the right to laugh:

ESTRAGON: We've no rights anymore?
VLADIMIR: You'd make me laugh if it wasn't prohibited.

Furthermore, they are reduced to crawling "on [their] hands and knees." Of course, in ancient cultures, man always approached a deity on his hands and knees. But in Beckett's dramas, a character's physical condition is correlated with his spiritual condition; all outward aspects of the two tramps reflect man's inward condition.

In a feeble attempt to assert their freedom, Estragon murmurs that they are not tied, but his assertion does not carry much conviction. The assertion, however feeble, that they are not tied might suggest man's revolt from God, because as soon as the idea of revolt is verbalized, they immediately hear a noise as though someone is approaching—Godot or God—to chastise them for heresy. They huddle together in fear:

> ESTRAGON: You gave me a fright.
> VLADIMIR: I thought it was he.
> ESTRAGON: Who?
> VLADIMIR: Godot.

After the discussion of whether or not they are tied has occupied their thoughts, Vladimir gives Estragon their last carrot to eat. Now they have only a turnip left to eat, and these reduced circumstances make it necessary for them to continue to wait for Godot—and possible salvation.

While eating his carrot, Estragon ruminates further about being "tied" or "ti-ed." Even though Vladimir feebly asserts that they are not tied, we noted that they are indeed tied to the idea of waiting. They cannot assert themselves; they have ceased struggling; there is even "no use wriggling." They are merely two stranded figures on an alien landscape who have given up struggling and are dependent upon waiting for Godot, realizing there is "nothing to be done." Thus, the play opens, and this section closes on the same note: *nothing to be done.*

ACT I: ARRIVAL OF POZZO AND LUCKY

As Vladimir and Estragon sit in peaceful resignation to their condition, a loud cry destroys the quietness and terrifies them. They immediately run to hide, huddling together and "cringing away from the menace." Suddenly Pozzo and Lucky arrive on the scene. Lucky has a rope around his neck and is being driven forward by Pozzo, who is brandishing a whip. This sudden, surprise entrance lacks only the flair of a drum roll and a band to give the entrance a highly theatrical, circus atmosphere. In the same way that Vladimir and Estragon are parodies of the circus clown or burlesque tramp, we now have the appearance of a character resembling a circus ringmaster and his trained animal. Throughout this scene, circus imagery is used to suggest that life itself can be seen as a circus, and one which will soon be brought to an abrupt end.

Vladimir and Estragon are in awe of the forceful manner in which Pozzo seems to be in control of Lucky; he seems to absolutely dominate the poor creature. Noting his *omnipotence* and *authority,* they inquire about the possibility of this man's being Godot. The mere fact that they have to ask, however, emphasizes their ignorance about the identity and true nature of Godot, the entity whom they are waiting for. They can't even explain Godot to Pozzo:

> VLADIMIR: . . . he's a kind of acquaintance.
> ESTRAGON: Personally, I wouldn't even know him if I saw him.

Throughout the scene, Pozzo conducts himself not only as a ringmaster, but also as a person far superior to the two tramps whom he condescends to spend some time with, even though he barely recognizes them as belonging to the same species. Furthermore, Vladimir and Estragon recognize Pozzo's seeming superiority and are dutifully obeisant to him, even after they discover that he is not Godot.

With the arrival of Pozzo and Lucky, we see how two people are *physically* tied to each other. Estragon and Vladimir are tied to each other by abstract bonds and also by their common act of waiting for Godot, but Lucky is literally and physically tied to Pozzo. And whereas Vladimir and Estragon are *waiting,* Pozzo and Lucky seem to be *going*—but where they are going is not stated.

After denying all knowledge of Godot, Pozzo magnanimously decides to rest for awhile. Even though Vladimir and Estragon are terribly inferior to him, Pozzo recognizes that they are "human beings none the less . . . of the same species as Pozzo! Made in God's image!" Thus, Pozzo recognizes these clowns (tramps) as belonging to the same species, albeit they are very imperfect specimens of the species, and he condescends to rest because he has been traveling for six hours without seeing a soul.

After rather elaborate preparations for settling himself, involving his ordering Lucky to set up a stool and picnic, Pozzo sits down to enjoy a meal of chicken and wine. Vladimir and Estragon begin an investigation of Lucky. Pozzo had earlier called the poor fellow "pig" and "hog." Vladimir, in particular, is appalled by Pozzo's treatment of Lucky and is quick to discover a running sore on Lucky's neck. The two conclude that Lucky is a "halfwit . . . a cretin." The irony here lies in the levels of humanity which Estragon and Vladimir fail to grasp—that is, Lucky is very much like Pozzo, and he is also very much like the tramps; he is a member of the same species, and his predicament emphasizes the essential oneness of us all.

After Pozzo has finished eating his chicken, Estragon notices the bones lying in the ditch and, to Vladimir's embarrassment, asks Pozzo if he can have the bones. Pozzo refers the matter to Lucky since Lucky has the first right to the bones. Lucky, however, ignores all the questions, and Estragon receives the bones. Meanwhile, Vladimir continues to be shocked by Pozzo's treatment of Lucky. He tries to express his horror over the situation only to be ignored. Vladimir wants to leave, but he is reminded that they must meet Godot.

Pozzo justifies his treatment of Lucky by maintaining that Lucky wants to impress him with his ability to carry things; yet, in reality, Lucky is very bad in that capacity. A basis of any relationship can be seen in Pozzo and Lucky's relationship, where one person has a desire to dominate and command and the other person craves to be dominated and to be a slave. Pozzo points out that the reverse could have easily been true—that he could have been, in other chance situations, Lucky's slave.

As Lucky begins to weep upon hearing that he might be sold at the fair and that the world would be a better place without him ("the best thing would be to kill . . . such creatures"), Pozzo notes that tears in themselves are not unusual: "The tears of the world are a constant quality. For each one who begins to weep, somewhere else another stops." Basically, for Beckett, the misery of human existence will always exist, and man must learn to live with his tears and his misery. For example, when Estragon tries to wipe away Lucky's tears, Lucky rewards him with a tremendous kick in the shins.

Estragon, Pozzo, and Vladimir talk in circles with images of the circus and the music hall dominating their conversation. Pozzo, feeling the need of leaving if he is to keep on his schedule, undertakes a lyrical explanation of "what our twilights can do." His recitation goes from lyrical enthusiasm about the nature of the gentleness of the "sky at this hour of the day" to a realization that more ominous matters lurk "behind this veil of gentleness and peace" and that, eventually, night "will burst upon us . . . when we least expect it . . . that's how it is on this bitch of an earth." The seriousness of this speech and its contents are then undermined when Pozzo lets it be known that he was merely delivering a pompous, memorized oration.

Before leaving, Pozzo wishes to express his appreciation to Vladimir and Estragon and wonders if they have any requests of him. Estragon immediately asks for ten francs (or even five, if ten is too much), but Vladimir interrupts and asserts that he and Estragon are not beggars. Pozzo then offers to let Lucky entertain them by dancing, singing, reciting, or thinking. They decide first on dancing and then on thinking.

ACT I: LUCKY'S DANCE AND SPEECH

Lucky's dance is merely a clumsy shuffling, which is a complete disappointment to Vladimir and Estragon. Thus they decide to have Lucky think. They give him his hat, and after protesting Pozzo's brutality, they arrange themselves for Lucky's performance of thinking. It takes the form of a long, seemingly incoherent speech. The speech is delivered as a set piece, yet it is anything but a set piece. Under different directors, this scene can be variously played. For example, Lucky most often speaks directly to the audience with the other characters at his back, while Vladimir and Estragon become more and more agitated as the speech progresses. Often Vladimir and Estragon run forward and try to stop Lucky from continuing his speech. As they try to stop Lucky, he delivers his oration in rapid-fire shouts. At times, Pozzo pulls on Lucky's rope, making it even more difficult for him to continue with his speech. The frenzied activity on the stage, the rapid delivery of the speech, and the jerking of the rope make it virtually impossible to tell anything at all about the speech and, consequently, emphasize the metaphysical absurdity of the entire performance. Lucky's speech is an incoherent jumble of words which seems to upset Vladimir and Estragon, for sporadically both rise to protest some element of the speech. Therefore, the speech does communicate *something* to the two

tramps or else they would not know to protest. The form of th
speech is that of a scholarly, theological address, beginning "Giver
the existence . . . of a personal God," but it is actually a parody of
this kind of address since the nonsensical and the absurd element
are in the foreground and the meaningful aspects of it are totally
obscured, as is the God whom Lucky discusses. Here, we have a
combination of the use of scholastic, theological terminology alon
with the absurd and the nonsensical. For example, the use of *qua* (a
Latin term meaning "in the function or capacity of") is common in
such scholarly addresses, but Lucky's repetition of the term as *qua*
quaquaqua creates an absurd, derisive sound, as though God i
being ridiculed by a quacking or squawking sound. Furthermore, th
speech is filled with various academic sounding words, some rea
words like *aphasia* (a loss of speech; here it refers to the fact tha
God from his divine heights now has divine aphasia or a divine si
lence) and some words like *apathia* or *athambia* which do not exis
(even though *apathia* is closely aligned to *apathy* and thus become
another oblique comment on the apathy of God in the universe)
Other absurd terms are used throughout the speech, and there i
also a frequent use of words which sound obscene, interspersed
throughout the speech. As an example, the names of the scholar
Fartov and Belcher are obviously created for their vulgarity.

Therefore, the speech is filled with more nonsense than sense—
more that is illogical than that which is logical. If, however, we re
move the illogical modifiers, irrelevancies, and incomprehensibl
statements and place them to the side, the essence of the speech i
as follows in the left-hand column:

THE ESSENCE OF LUCKY'S SPEECH	THE IRRELEVANCIES THE ABSURDITIES
"Given [acknowledging] the existence . . .	
	as uttered forth in the public works of Puncher and Wattmann
of a personal God . . .	with white beard quaquaquaqua
[who exists] outside [of] time . . .	
	without extension
[and] who . . .	from the heights of divine apathi divine athambia divine aphasia
	with some exceptions . . .
loves us dearly . . .	but time will tell [etc.]
	like the divine Miranda [etc.]
and [who] suffers . . .	

with those who . . .	for reasons unknown, but time will tell
are plunged in torment . . .	in fire [etc.] [that will] blast hell to heaven so blue . . . so calm [etc.]
it is established beyond all doubt . . .	all other doubt than that which clings to the labors of men that as a result of the labors [etc.]
that man . . .	in short
that man . . .	in spite of the strides of alimentation and defecation, wastes [etc.]
for reasons unknown . . .	no matter what the facts [etc.]
for reasons unknown . . .	in spite of the tennis [etc.]
for reasons unknown . . .	in spite of the tennis on on the beard [etc.]
[our] labors abandoned left unfinished . . .	graver still [etc.]
abandoned unfinished . . .	the skull the skull in Connemara [etc.]

Lucky's speech is an attempt, however futile, to make a statement about man and God. Reduced to its essence, the speech is basically as follows:

> acknowledging the existence of a personal God, one who exists outside of time and who loves us dearly and who suffers with those who are plunged into torment, it is established beyond all doubt that man, for reasons unknown, has left his labors abandoned, unfinished.

It is significant that the speech ends at this point because man can make certain assumptions about God and create certain hypotheses about God, *but* man can never come to a logical conclusion about God. One must finish a discourse about God, as Lucky did, by repeating "for reasons unknown . . . for reasons unknown . . . for reasons unknown. . . ." And equally important is the fact that any statement made about God is, by its nature, lost in a maze of irrelevance, absurdity, and incoherence—without an ending. Therefore, man's final comment about God can amount to nothing more than a bit of garbled noise which contains no coherent statement and no conclusion. Furthermore, Lucky's utterances are stopped only after he is physically overpowered by the others.

After the speech, Pozzo tries to revive Lucky, who is emotionally exhausted, completely enervated by his speech. After great difficulty, Pozzo gets Lucky up, and amid protracted adieus, he begins to go, albeit he begins to go the wrong way. Pozzo's inability to leave suggests man's reliance upon others and his natural instinct to cling to someone else. But with one final adieu, Pozzo and Lucky depart.

ACT I: DEPARTURE OF POZZO AND LUCKY: VLADIMIR AND ESTRAGON ALONE

With the departure of Pozzo and Lucky, Vladimir realizes that he is glad that the episode helped pass the time. Constantly, the two are faced with finding some way of passing the time while waiting, even though Estragon philosophically points out that time "would have passed in any case." Thus the entire episode seemingly has no real significance to them. They return to wondering what they can do now—besides wait for Godot. Since they can do nothing, they decide to make a little conversation about whether or not they had previously known Pozzo and Lucky, but no agreement is reached. Estragon then returns to tending his aching feet.

ACT I: ARRIVAL OF BOY MESSENGER

Out of nowhere a boy with a message from Mr. Godot appears, but the boy is too frightened to come close to the tramps. They question the boy about his fears and ask him if he has been here before. Suddenly, the boy delivers his message: "Mr. Godot told me to tell you he won't come this evening, but surely to-morrow." The tramps question the boy about Mr. Godot and discover that the boy tends the goats for Mr. Godot, that Mr. Godot does not beat him, but that he does beat the boy's brother, who tends the sheep. Both of the brothers sleep in the hayloft of the barn. The boy then leaves.

The main significance of the arrival of the boy lies in what light he can shed on the figure of Godot. By the way the tramps question the boy about Godot, we now realize that Vladimir and Estragon know very little, if anything, about Godot. Apparently, Godot keeps sheep and goats and is good to the boy who tends the goats but beats the brother who tends the sheep. The reasons for beating the brother are unknown. If, therefore, Godot is equated with God, then Godot's behavior would suggest an Old Testament God who accepts the offering of one brother (Abel) and rejects the offering of the other brother (Cain). God's rejection of Cain's offering is difficult or impossible to explain. Thus Godot's actions are as incomprehensible as some of the actions of the Old Testament God.

ACT I: VLADIMIR AND ESTRAGON ALONE

After the boy leaves, Vladimir and Estragon are left alone. Night has fallen and the moon has risen. The two tramps resolve to leave since there is "nothing to do here," but then, hopefully, Vladimir reminds Estragon that the boy said "Godot was sure to come to-morrow." Thus, they must wait—even though nothing is certain. Impulsively, they decide to leave—but do not do so.

The first act ends as it began. Estragon is still concerned about his feet and his boots, which he is now carrying. Vladimir reminds Estragon that he can't go barefoot because it's too cold, and Estragon compares his going barefoot with Christ's going barefoot. Vladimir can't see the comparison; Christ went barefoot in a *warm* climate. Yet Estragon is quick to point out that it was precisely because of that warm climate that Christ was crucified quickly, whereas here and now, man, by implication, must suffer for an extended time. The futility of their situation makes Estagon wish for some rope so that he can hang himself. The thought of death reminds him of a time about fifty years ago when he threw himself in the Rhone River and was "fished out" by Vladimir. This allusion reminds us of the Christian symbols of baptism, cleansing, and renewal. Yet the incident occurred fifty years ago, so now it is "all dead and buried." In other words, there is no more hope of baptism and renewal—instead, they must face the coldness and the darkness of the world alone.

The first act began with the line "Nothing to be done." Nothing has been done. Now Vladimir and Estragon realize that "nothing is certain," and that "nothing is worth while now." Consequently, they decide: "Let's go." But instead, according to the stage directions, *"They do not move."* The act ends, therefore, with a contradiction between their words and their actions. All they can do now is simply wait.

ACT II: VLADIMIR AND ESTRAGON ALONE

The second act begins almost exactly as the first act did—with one exception: there are now four or five leaves on the once barren tree. As in Act I, Estragon is alone and Vladimir enters, singing some repetitious doggerel about a dog which was beaten to death because he stole a crust of bread. The repetition of the doggerel is typical of the repetition of the entire drama, and the condition of the dog in the doggerel is similar to the condition of the two tramps. Again, as in Act I, Vladimir wonders where Estragon spent the night and discovers that Estragon has again been beaten. Thus, the dog in the doggerel was beaten to death, and now we hear that Estragon is suffering from a beating. Consequently, the second act begins on a note of death, but one that is doubly ominous.

After a moment, the two tramps are reconciled and embrace each other, pretending that all is right between them. However, Estragon immediately reminds Vladimir that he was singing all the while that he (Estragon) was being beaten. Vladimir can only respond that "one is not master of one's moods." Vladimir's remarks characterize the actions of the first act—especially where it was evident that the two tramps were not in control of their lives, that they were unable to determine what was going to happen to them.

We now discover part of the reason for Vladimir's singing. He is happy because he slept all night long. The urinary trouble that he had in the first act did not force him to get up during the night and, therefore, he enjoyed a complete night's sleep. But then, if Vladimir had been with Estragon, he would not have let the people beat Estragon. Vladimir assumes a traditional philosophical position, a position that goes back to the writer of the Book of Job in the Old Testament. If Estragon was beaten, it was because he was guilty of doing something wrong and, had Vladimir been with Estragon, he would have stopped him from doing whatever it was that caused Estragon to get a beating. This scene reminds one of Franz Kafka's *The Trial*; there, the main character is punished for a crime and is never able to discover what his crime was and feels increasingly more guilty by asking what he is accused of.

After the two convince each other that they are happy, they then settle down to wait for Godot, and the basic refrain of the drama reemerges: the two tramps can do nothing but wait. Suddenly, Vladimir is aware that "things have changed here since yesterday." The change that Vladimir notices (and note that it is always Vladimir who is the most perceptive of the two, even though in the final analysis he is also incapable of changing their predicament) concerns the tree. Later, the change in the tree will be more fully appreciated, but for now, Estragon is not convinced that it is the same tree; he does not even remember if it is the same tree that they nearly hanged themselves from yesterday. In addition, Estragon has almost forgotten the appearance of Pozzo and Lucky, except for the bone he was given to gnaw on. Blankly, he asks, "all that was yesterday, you say?" For Estragon, time has no real meaning; his only concern with time is that it is something to be used up while waiting for Godot. He dismisses the discussion by pointing out that the world about him is a "muckheap" from which he has never stirred.

The world-as-a-muckheap is a central image in Beckett's work— for example, in *Endgame*, one of the central images is garbage cans as symbols of the status of man, who belongs on the refuse heap of the world. Estragon solidifies the image of the world-as-a-muckheap by asking Vladimir to tell him about worms.

In contrast to the landscape, or world which they now inhabit, Vladimir reminds Estragon of a time once long ago when they lived in the Macon country and picked grapes for someone whose name he can't remember. But it has been so long ago that Estragon can't remember and can only assert that he "has puked [his] puke of a life away here . . . in the Cackon country!" The oblique reference to another time and place where apparently grapes (the biblical symbol of fertility) could be harvested contrasts with this barren landscape where they now eat dried tubers of turnips and radishes. If Estragon and Vladimir are representatives of mankind waiting for God to appear to them, then we realize that possibly they are in this barren land because they represent man as fallen man—man who has been cast out of the Garden of Eden, man who originally was picking the grapes of God has now incurred the wrath of God, who refuses to appear to them any more.

Vladimir and Estragon make a desperate attempt at conversation in order to make time pass "so we won't think." Their efforts at conversation are strained and useless, and each time after a few meaningless words, they obey the stage directions: *Silence*. This is repeated ten times within the passing of a minute or so—that is, a few meaningless phrases are uttered, followed by "silences." The two even contemplate trying to contradict each other, but even that fails. The entire passage is characterized by a brooding sense of helplessness and melancholy. The images are those of barren, sterile lifelessness—the falling of leaves, ashes, dead voices, skeletons, corpses, and charnel-houses, etc. All of these images are juxtaposed to the background idea of a once-fertile life "in the Macon country" that can no longer be remembered and the idea that they are constantly involved in the sterile, unprofitable endeavor of waiting for Godot. The entire conversation is absolutely pointless, and yet Estragon responds, "Yes, but now we'll have to find something else." The only effect, then, of their banter was to pass the time.

With nothing else to do, the two tramps are momentarily diverted when Vladimir discovers that the tree which was "all black and bare" yesterday evening is now "covered with leaves." This leads to a discussion of whether or not the two tramps are in the same place; after all, it would be impossible for a tree to sprout leaves overnight. Perhaps it has been longer than just yesterday when they were here. Yet Vladimir points out Estragon's wounded leg; that is proof that they were here yesterday.

The confusion about time and place is typical of Beckett's dramas. How long the two tramps have been in this particular place can never be determined. The fact that Estragon has a wound proves nothing because man is eternally wounded in Beckett's dramas and, furthermore, can show proof of his injuries. The leaves on the tree, which earlier was black and bare, astonish Vladimir. It would indeed be a miracle if such an event could occur in a single night, and this would open up all types of opportunities for miracles to occur. But the discussion of a miracle is rejected by Estragon because the leaves have no mystical appearance. They could be a manifestation of spring, or else this could be an entirely different tree. Consequently, their conversation is inconclusive, and we never know if this is the same tree in the same place or not. This confusion is characteristic of Vladimir and Estragon's inability to cope with life.

As Vladimir is trying to prove to Estragon that Pozzo and Lucky were here yesterday, he makes Estragon pull up his trousers so that they can both see the wound which is "beginning to fester." This scene is especially significant in the manner that it is staged because the actions of the two tramps are those found in a burlesque comedy house, with Vladimir holding up Estragon's leg while Estragon can hardly keep his balance, and against this background of farcical comedy is the contrasting intellectual idea of the metaphysical and spiritual wounds that man carries about with him.

The wound on Estragon's leg, in turn, causes Vladimir to notice that Estragon does not have his boots on. Coincidentally, there is a pair of boots lying on the ground, but Estragon maintains that his boots were black and this pair is brown. Maybe someone came and exchanged boots. Are they the same boots or someone else's boots?

As with the tree, the confusion about the boots is a further indication of the inadequacy of Estragon and Vladimir's logic and reasoning. They are unable to find anything which will help "give us the impression that we exist." The boots were to be objective proof of their particular existence on this particular bit of landscape at this particular time, but in an absurdly tragic manner, they cannot even determine if the boots are the same boots that existed yesterday. They are unable to find within themselves or outside themselves anything which is helpful in establishing their existences. There is no hope within or without. Therefore, even the attempt to arrive at a conclusion totally exhausts them, and with the familiar refrain "we are waiting for Godot," they abandon the problem.

But the boots are still there, and Vladimir convinces Estragon to try them on. Even though they are too big, Estragon grudgingly admits that the boots do fit him. Then with his new boots on, Estragon wishes that he could sleep. "He resumes his foetal posture" and to the accompaniment of a lullaby sung by Vladimir, Estragon is soon asleep, only to be awakened shortly by the recurrence of a nightmare. Frightened, Estragon wishes to leave, but Vladimir reminds him that they can't leave because they are "waiting for Godot."

Estragon's assuming the fetal position suggests his complete resignation and despair, his defeat in the face of such staggering, unsolvable metaphysical problems as the significance of the tree and the mysterious boots. Obviously, too, this is a "return-to-the-womb" situation wherein Estragon can escape from the responsibilities of life. His security in the womb, however, does not last long because he is awakened by a nightmare about falling. Whether it is a nightmare involving falling from the womb (man's most traumatic physical experience) or falling from God's grace (man's most traumatic spiritual experience), we are never sure.

Suddenly, Estragon can bear no more. He is going and tells Vladimir that he will never see him again. Vladimir doesn't pay attention, for he has found a hat, Lucky's hat; and so, in the midst of all these ambiguous physical and philosophical considerations, we have another burlesque interlude. In the tradition of the old burlesque theater, a tramp (Vladimir) in an old bowler hat discovers another hat on the ground. There follows an exchange-of-hats act between himself and his partner that could be found in many burlesque acts. The hat is apparently the one that Lucky left the day before, during the scene when he was silenced after his speech. The comic exchange begins when Vladimir gives his own hat to Estragon and replaces it with Lucky's. Estragon then does the same, offering his hat to Vladimir, who replaces it for Lucky's, and hands Lucky's hat to Estragon, who replaces it for Vladimir's and so on until they tire of the interchange. And then there is silence.

Once more the two tramps must pass the time while waiting. They decide to play a game of pretending to be Pozzo and Lucky, but this game lasts only a moment because they think that they hear someone approaching. After a frantic search for some place to hide, they decide that there is no one coming. Vladimir then tells Estragon: "You must have had a vision," a phrase that is reminiscent of T. S. Eliot's *The Love Song of J. Alfred Prufrock*, a long poem in which the main character, an ineffectual intellectual of the twentieth century, cannot do anything, much less have the strength to have visions. Furthermore, visions are associated with people entirely different from these two tramps. To think that they could have a vision is absurd.

One more game is attempted. Remembering Pozzo's calling Lucky ugly names and recalling the anger and frustration of the master and his slave, they begin a game of name-calling. It is Vladimir who suggests the idea of the game: "Let's abuse each other." There follows in rapid succession a series of name-calling:

VLADIMIR: Moron!
ESTRAGON: Vermin!
VLADIMIR: Abortion!
ESTRAGON: Morpion!
VLADIMIR: Sewer-rat!
ESTRAGON: Curate!
VLADIMIR: Cretin!

After this, they make up, and then they decide to exercise, mutually relieved by the discovery that time flies when one "has fun!"

VLADIMIR: We could do our exercises.
ESTRAGON: Our movements.
VLADIMIR: Our elevations.

ESTRAGON: Our relaxations.
VLADIMIR: Our elongations.
[etc., etc.]

The name-calling, the embracing, and the exercising are finally over; they have been no more than futile attempts to pass the time while waiting for Godot, and Estragon is reduced to flailing his fists and crying at the top of his voice, "God have pity on me! . . . On me! On me! Pity! On me!"

ACT II: ARRIVAL OF POZZO AND LUCKY

Suddenly and without warning, as in the first act, Pozzo and Lucky come back on stage. Their arrival puts an end to Vladimir and Estragon's games. Things have changed significantly for Pozzo and Lucky. The long rope which bound them together is now much shorter, binding them closer together and suggesting that however much man might consider himself to be different from others, ultimately he is drawn or bound closer and closer. Furthermore, Pozzo and Lucky are physically changed: Pozzo is blind and Lucky is dumb (i.e., mute). But the entire scene is played without the audience's knowing that Lucky is now dumb. As they enter, staggering under their load, Lucky now carries suitcases filled with sand (symbolically, perhaps, the sands of time). Lucky falls and drags Pozzo down with him.

With the arrival of Pozzo and Lucky, Vladimir and Estragon think that help ("reinforcements") have arrived from Godot. But they soon realize that it is just Pozzo and Lucky. Estragon wants to leave then, but Vladimir must remind him once again that they cannot go; they are "waiting for Godot." After some consideration, Vladimir decides that they should help Pozzo and Lucky get up. But Estragon wants to consider an alternative plan. After all, he was wounded by Lucky the day before. Vladimir reminds him, however, that "it is not everyday that we are needed." This is one of the most profound comments of the drama. Vladimir realizes that Pozzo's cries for help were addressed to "all of mankind," and "at this place, at this moment of time, all mankind is us, whether we like it or not." This statement certainly clarifies the idea that Vladimir and Estragon represent all mankind in its relationship to God (Godot). Realizing this, Vladimir also realizes that man's fate is to be a part of "the foul brood to which a cruel fate consigned us."

Instead of Hamlet's "To be or not to be, that is the question," Vladimir asks, "What are we doing here, *that* is the question." Again, his problem is more akin to the dilemma of T. S. Eliot's Prufrock (who is also faced with an "overwhelming question": should he marry or not?) than it is to the predicament of Shakespeare's Hamlet. Vladimir concludes: "We [all mankind] are waiting for Godot to come." Hamlet's metaphysical question about existence is reduced to a Prufrockian decision to do nothing but wait.

At the end of Vladimir's speech, Pozzo's call for help loses importance as Vladimir once again asserts his pride in the fact that they have at least kept their appointment to meet Godot; not all people can make such a boast. Vladimir's confusing the metaphysical with the practical anticipates the confused actions that are to immediately follow—that is, Vladimir decides that they should help Pozzo and Lucky get up, and the result is that all four of the men ultimately end up on the ground. Thus their cries for help fall on deaf ears.

The entire scene in which the two tramps try to help two equally distraught figures get up returns the drama to the burlesque house. The scene is a parody of many similar types of scenes found in burlesque theaters, thus emphasizing again the absurdity of man's actions, or in the words of Estragon: "We are all born mad. Some remain so."

Immediately after the above statement, Estragon leaves off with philosophy and becomes very practical; he wants to know how much Pozzo is willing to pay to be extricated from his position. Meanwhile, Vladimir is concerned with finding something to do to pass the time: "We are bored to death"; he begins his efforts to help Pozzo, but, as noted above, they all end up in a heap on the ground, and Pozzo, in fear, "extricates himself," then crawls away. This incident also serves as a contrast to Pozzo's actions in the first act; there, he was proud and disdainful and asserted himself with aloofness and superiority. Now he has lost all his previous qualities and is simply a pathetic, blind figure crawling about on the ground. Like Job or Sophocles' blind Oedipus, Pozzo seems to suggest that no man's life can be secure since tomorrow might bring incalculable catastrophes.

Lying on the ground, Vladimir and Estragon try to call to Pozzo, who doesn't answer. Then Estragon decides to call him by some other name:

> ESTRAGON: . . . try [calling] him with other names. . . . It'd pass the time. And we'd be bound to hit on the right one sooner or later.
> VLADIMIR: I tell you his name is Pozzo.
> ESTRAGON: We'll soon see. (*He reflects*.) Abel! Abel!
> POZZO: Help!
> ESTRAGON: Got it in one!
> VLADIMIR: I begin to weary of this motif.
> ESTRAGON: Perhaps the other is called Cain. Cain! Cain!
> POZZO: Help!
> ESTRAGON: He's all humanity.

Beckett's use of the names of Abel and Cain stresses the universality of the characters since Pozzo answers to both names. According to some interpretations of the scriptures, all of mankind carries with it both the mark of Cain and the mark of Abel; thus Pozzo can answer to both names because "He's all humanity!"

To pass the time, Estragon suggests that they stand up. They do. Then Estragon suggests once again, "Let's go," only to be reminded once again that they must remain because "we're waiting for Godot."

Since there is nothing else to do, Vladimir and Estragon help Pozzo get up. It is then that they discover that he is blind. In contrast to the Pozzo of the first act, we now see a pathetic figure leaning on the two tramps for physical support and pleading for help because he is blind. For Estragon, there is hope in Pozzo's blindness because the prophets of old, such as the Greek Tiresias, were often blind but could "see into the future," exactly what Estragon hopes Pozzo can do. But there is no hope for Vladimir and Estragon. Carrying through with the Greek imagery, Estragon tires of holding Pozzo, especially since he can't prophesy for them. Pozzo wants to drop him since he and Vladimir "are not caryatids" (caryatids were statues of Greek goddesses used to hold up temples; why Estragon uses this word instead of "telamons," the male equivalent, is confusing).

Because of his blindness, Pozzo has also lost all contact with time. He even refuses to answer questions about what happened yesterday: "The blind have no notion of time." This confusion over time is symptomatic of his changed condition; just as he has lost all contact with life, so also has time lost all significance for him. When Vladimir hears that Lucky is dumb, he inquires, "Since when?" The question incenses Pozzo and causes him to violently reject Vladimir's concern with time: "Have you not done tormenting me with your accursed time! It's abominable! When! When! One day, is that not enough for you, one day he went dumb, one day I went blind, one day we'll go deaf, one day we were born, one day we shall die, the same day, the same second, is that not enough for you?" For Pozzo, one day at a time is enough for him to cope with. All he knows now and all that he "sees" now is the misery of life. Life itself is only a brief moment—that flash of light between the darkness of the womb and of the tomb. "They give birth astride of a grave, the light gleams an instant, then it's night once more." Thus the grave-digger is the midwife of mankind. Ending on this note of utter despair, Pozzo arouses Lucky and they struggle off to continue on their journey.

ACT II: DEPARTURE OF POZZO AND LUCKY: VLADIMIR AND ESTRAGON ALONE

While Vladimir and Pozzo have been talking, Estragon has been sleeping again in his fetal position. Vladimir, feeling lonely, awakens him. Significantly, since Estragon was sleeping in his fetal position, his dreams were happy ones; but even so, Vladimir refuses to listen to them. Vladimir's final speech before the entrance of the Boy Messenger suggests that he feels a deep estrangement from the universe. Something tells him that there should be some reason for him to be here—at this place, at this time, with his friend Estragon while waiting for Godot. Furthermore, he is aware of a misery, a disquietness which he cannot understand. Life seems as though it is "astride of a grave," and there is to be a "difficult birth," for the "grave-digger puts on the forceps." Vladimir senses that life is filled with the cries of a suffering humanity, but he has used "a great deadener" (boredom) as a barrier to these cries. Suddenly, in complete despair, he cries out: "I can't go on." But the alternative to his despair is obviously death; therefore, he immediately rejects his despair by asking, "What have I said?" There is left only man's stubborn, useless clinging to a meaningless life.

ACT II: ARRIVAL OF BOY MESSENGER

Vladimir's depression is suddenly interrupted by the appearance of a boy. Since this boy asserts that he was not here yesterday, he has to be a different one. However, the message that he brings is identical to the one brought yesterday by a boy: Mr. Godot will not come this evening but he will surely come tomorrow, without fail. Thus Vladimir finds that there is absolutely nothing to do but wait for Godot. But in view of the message from the boy of the preceding day, the assurance that Godot will come tomorrow is lacking in conviction.

Upon questioning the boy further, Vladimir discovers two things —that Mr. Godot "does nothing" and that he has a white beard. Since God is sometimes viewed as a Supreme Entity doing nothing and possessing a long white beard, then if Godot is God, there can be little or no hope for God's intervention in the affairs of men. Instead, man must continue to stumble through this muckheap, this ash can of a world. Vladimir tells the boy to inform Mr. Godot that "you saw me." Vladimir is so insistent on the fact that the boy has indeed seen him that he makes "a sudden spring forward." This frightens the boy, and he quickly runs offstage.

ACT II: DEPARTURE OF BOY MESSENGER: VLADIMIR AND ESTRAGON ALONE

After the boy leaves, the sun sets and the moon rises, indicating that another day of waiting for Godot has passed. Estragon awakens and wants to leave this desolate place, but Vladimir reminds him that they have to wait for Godot. When Estragon suggests that they "drop Godot" and leave, Vladimir reminds Estragon that if they did, Godot would "punish us."

As he did at the end of Act I, Estragon once again brings up the subject of their hanging themselves. But Estragon forgot to bring the rope. They decide to hang themselves with the cord that holds up Estragon's trousers, but when tested, the cord breaks. This misadventure returns us to the world of the circus and the world of the burlesque house, and this rare, decisive action to kill themselves is rendered ludicrous since in the process of testing the cord, Estragon suffers the indignity of having his trousers fall down. Thus we see again Beckett's notion of the incongruity between what man attempts (and longs to be) and the absurdity of his position and his actions.

Since they have to come back tomorrow to wait for Godot, Estragon once again proposes that they bring "a good bit of rope" with them; Vladimir agrees:

> VLADIMIR: We'll hang ourselves tomorrow. (Pause) Unless Godot comes.
> ESTRAGON: And if he comes?
> VLADIMIR: We'll be saved.

The question then is: if Godot doesn't come, will Vladimir and Estragon be damned?

After telling Estragon to put on his trousers, which are still around his ankles since the cord that held up his trousers is now broken, Vladimir suggests that they leave:

> VLADIMIR: Well? Shall we go?
> ESTRAGON: Yes, let's go.
> *They do not move.*

Curtain

The ending of Act II is exactly the same as was the ending of Act I, and we have one final example of the disparity between the characters' words and the characters' actions. And since both acts are so identical and so circular, it should be obvious that tomorrow will find the two tramps back at the same place waiting for Godot, who will not come but who will send a boy messenger to tell them that Godot will surely come tomorrow and they must come back to wait for Godot, etc., etc.

THE PLAY'S CIRCULAR STRUCTURE

"But what does it all mean?" is the most frequent statement heard after one has seen or finished reading a play from the Theater of the Absurd movement. Beckett's plays were among the earliest and, therefore, created a great deal of confusion among the early critics.

No definite conclusion or resolution can ever be offered to *Waiting for Godot* because the play is essentially circular and repetitive in nature. Once again, turn to the Dramatic Divisions section in these Notes and observe that the structure of each act is exactly alike. A traditional play, in contrast, has an introduction of the characters and the exposition; then, there is a statement of the problem of the play in relationship to its settings and characters. (In *Waiting for Godot*, we never know where the play takes place, except that it is set on "a country road.") Furthermore, in a traditional play, the characters are developed, and gradually we come to see the dramatist's world view; the play then rises to a climax, and there is a conclusion. This type of development is called a linear development. In the plays of the Theater of the Absurd, the structure is often exactly the opposite. We have, instead, a circular structure, and most aspects of this drama support this circular structure in one way or another.

The setting is the same, and the time is the same in both acts. Each act begins early in the morning, just as the tramps are awakening, and both acts close with the moon having risen. The action takes place in exactly the same landscape—a lonely, isolated road with one single tree. (In the second act, there are some leaves on the tree, but from the viewpoint of the audience, the setting is exactly the same.) We are never told where this road is located; all we know is that the action of the play unfolds on this lonely road. Thus, from Act I to Act II, there is no difference in either the setting or in the time and, thus, instead of a progression of time within an identifiable setting, we have a repetition in the second act of the same things that we saw and heard in the first act.

More important than the repetition of setting and time, however, is the repetition of the actions. To repeat, in addition to the basic structure of actions indicated earlier—that is:

> Vladimir and Estragon Alone
> Arrival of Pozzo and Lucky
> Vladimir and Estragon Alone
> Arrival of Boy Messenger
> Vladimir and Estragon Alone

there are many lesser actions that are repeated in both acts. At the beginning of each act, for example, several identical concerns should be noted. Among these is the emphasis on Estragon's boots. Also, too, Vladimir, when first noticing Estragon, uses virtually the same words: "So there you are again" in Act I and "There you are again" in Act II. At the beginning of both acts, the first discussion concerns a beating that Estragon received just prior to their meeting. At the beginning of both acts, Vladimir and Estragon emphasize repeatedly that they are there to wait for Godot. In the endings of both acts, Vladimir and Estragon discuss the possibility of hanging themselves, and in both endings they decide to bring some good strong rope with them the next day so that they can indeed hang themselves. In addition, both acts end with the same words, voiced differently:

ACT I: ESTRAGON: Well, shall we go?
        VLADIMIR: Yes, let's go.

ACT II: VLADIMIR: Well? Shall we go?
        ESTRAGON: Yes, let's go.

And the stage directions following these lines are exactly the same in each case: "*They do not move.*"

With the arrival of Pozzo and Lucky in each act, we notice that even though their physical appearance has theoretically changed, outwardly they seem the same; they are still tied together on an endless journey to an unknown place to rendezvous with a nameless person.

Likewise, the Boy Messenger, while theoretically different, brings the exact same message: Mr. Godot will not come today, but he will surely come tomorrow.

Vladimir's difficulties with urination and his suffering are discussed in each act as a contrast to the suffering of Estragon because of his boots. In addition, the subject of eating, involving carrots, radishes, and turnips, becomes a central image in each act, and the tramps' involvement with hats, their multiple insults, and their reconciling embraces—these and many more lesser matters are found repeatedly in both acts.

Finally, and most important, there are the larger concepts: first, the suffering of the tramps; second, their attempts, however futile, to pass time; third, their attempts to part, and, ultimately, their incessant waiting for Godot—all these make the two acts clearly repetitive, circular in structure, and the fact that these repetitions are so obvious in the play is Beckett's manner of breaking away from the traditional play and of asserting the uniqueness of his own circular structure.

CHARACTER ANALYSES

Vladimir and Estragon

In spite of the existential concept that man cannot take the essence of his existence from someone else, in viewing this play, we have to view Vladimir and Estragon in their relationship to each other. In fact, the novice viewing this play for the first time often fails to note any significant difference between the two characters. In hearing the play read, even the most experienced theater person will often confuse one of the characters for the other. Therefore, the similarities are as important as the differences between them.

Both are tramps dressed in costumes which could be interchanged. They both wear big boots which don't necessarily fit and both have big bowler hats. Their suits are baggy and ill-fitting. (In Act II, when Estragon removes the cord he uses for a belt, his trousers are so baggy that they fall about his feet.) Their costumes recall the type found in burlesque or vaudeville houses, the type often associated with the character of the "Little Tramp," portrayed by Charlie Chaplin.

The Chaplinesque-type costume prepares us for many of the comic routines that Vladimir and Estragon perform. The opening scene with Estragon struggling with his boots and Vladimir doffing and donning his hat to inspect it for lice could be a part of a burlesque routine. The resemblance of their costumes to Chaplin's supports the view that these tramps are outcasts from society, but have the same plucky defiance to continue to exist as Chaplin's "Little Tramp" did.

Another action which could come directly from the burlesque theater occurs when Vladimir finds a hat on the ground which he tries on, giving his own to Estragon, who tries it on while giving his hat to Vladimir, who tries it on while giving the new-found hat to Estragon, who tries it on, etc. This comic episode continues until the characters—and the audience—are bored with it. Other burlesque-like scenes involve Vladimir's struggles to help Estragon with his boots while Estragon is hopping awkwardly about the stage on one foot to keep from falling; another scene involves the loss of Estragon's pants, while other scenes involve the two tramps' grotesque efforts to help Pozzo and Lucky get up off the ground and their inept attempts to hang themselves. Thus, the two characters are tied together partly by being two parts of a burlesque act.

Vladimir

In any comic or burlesque act, there are two characters, traditionally known as the "straight man" and the "fall guy." Vladimir would be the equivalent of the straight man. He is also the intellectual who is concerned with a variety of ideas. Of the two, Vladimir makes the decisions and remembers significant aspects of their past. He is the one who constantly reminds Estragon that they must wait for Godot. Even though it is left indefinite, all implications suggest that Vladimir knows more about Godot than does Estragon, who tells us that he has never even seen Godot and thus has no idea what Godot looks like.

Vladimir is the one who often sees religious or philosophical implications in their discussions of events, and he interprets their actions in religious terms; for example, he is concerned about the religious implications in such stories as the two thieves (two tramps) who were crucified on either side of Jesus. He is troubled about the fate of the thief who wasn't saved and is concerned that "only one of the four evangelists" speaks of a thief being saved.

Vladimir correlates some of their actions to the general concerns of mankind. In Act II, when Pozzo and Lucky fall down and cry for help, Vladimir interprets their cries for help as his and Estragon's chance to be in a unique position of helping humanity. After all, Vladimir maintains, "It is not everyday that we are needed . . . but at this place, at this moment in time," they are needed and should respond to the cries for help. Similarly, it is Vladimir who questions Pozzo and Lucky and the Boy Messenger(s), while Estragon remains, for the most part, the silent listener. Essentially, Vladimir must constantly remind Estragon of their destiny—that is, they must wait for Godot.

In addition to the larger needs, Vladimir also looks after their physical needs. He helps Estragon with his boots, and, moreover, had he been with Estragon at night, he would not have allowed his friend to be beaten; also, he looks after and rations their meager meals of turnips, carrots, and radishes, and, in general, he tends to be the manager of the two.

Estragon

In contrast, Estragon is concerned mainly with more mundane matters: he prefers a carrot to a radish or turnip, his feet hurt, and he blames his boots; he constantly wants to leave, and it must be drilled into him that he *must* wait for Godot. He remembers that he was beaten, but he sees no philosophical significance in the beating. He is willing to beg for money from a stranger (Pozzo), and he eats Pozzo's discarded chicken bones with no shame.

Estragon, then, is the more basic of the two. He is not concerned with either religious or philosophical matters. First of all, he has never even heard of the two thieves who were crucified with Christ, and if the Gospels do disagree, then "that's all there is to it," and any further discussion is futile and absurd.

Estragon's basic nature is illustrated in Act II when he shows so little interest in Pozzo and Lucky that he falls asleep; also, he sleeps through the entire scene between Vladimir and the Boy Messenger. He is simply not concerned with such issues.

Estragon, however, is dependent upon Vladimir, and essentially he performs what Vladimir tells him to do. For example, Vladimir looks after Estragon's boots, he rations out the carrots, turnips, and radishes, he comforts Estragon's pain, and he reminds Estragon of their need to wait for Godot. Estragon does sometimes suggest that it would be better if they parted, but he never leaves Vladimir for long. Essentially, Estragon is the less intelligent one; he has to have everything explained to him, and he is essentially so bewildered by life that he has to have someone to look after him.

Pozzo and Lucky

Together they represent the antithesis of each other. Yet they are strongly and irrevocably tied together—both physically and metaphysically. Any number of polarities could be used to apply to them. If Pozzo is the master (and father figure), then Lucky is the slave (or child). If Pozzo is the circus ringmaster, then Lucky is the trained or performing animal. If Pozzo is the sadist; Lucky is the masochist. Or Pozzo can be seen as the Ego and Lucky as the Id. An inexhaustible number of polarities can be suggested.

Pozzo

Pozzo appears on stage after the appearance of Lucky. They are tied together by a long rope; thus, their destinies are fixed together in the same way that Pozzo might be a mother figure, with the rope being the umbilical cord which ties the two together.

Everything about Pozzo resembles our image of the circus ringmaster. If the ringmaster is the chief person of the circus, then it is no wonder that Vladimir and Estragon first mistook him for Godot or God. Like a ringmaster, he arrives brandishing a whip, which is the trademark of the professional. In fact, we hear the cracking of Pozzo's whip before we actually see him. Also, a stool is often associated with an animal trainer, and Pozzo constantly calls Lucky by animal terms or names. Basically, Pozzo commands and Lucky obeys.

In the first act, Pozzo is immediately seen in terms of this authoritarian figure. He lords over the others, and he is decisive, powerful, and confident. He gives the illusion that he knows exactly where he is going and exactly how to get there. He seems "on top" of every situation.

When he arrives on the scene and sees Vladimir and Estragon, he recognizes them as human, but as inferior beings; then he condescendingly acknowledges that there is a human likeness, even though the "likeness is an imperfect one." This image reinforces his authoritarian god-like stance: we are made in God's image but imperfectly so. Pozzo's superiority is also seen in the manner in which he eats the chicken, then casts the bones to Lucky with an air of complete omnipotence.

In contrast to the towering presence exhibited by Pozzo in Act I, a significant change occurs between the two acts. The rope is shortened, drawing Pozzo much closer to his antithesis, Lucky. Pozzo is now blind; he cannot find his way alone. He stumbles and falls. He cannot get along without help; he is pathetic. He can no longer command. Rather than driving Lucky as he did earlier, he is now pathetically dragged along by Lucky. From a position of omnipotence and strength and confidence, he has fallen and has become the complete fallen man who maintains that time is irrelevant and that man's existence is meaningless. Unlike the great blind prophets of yore who could see everything, for Pozzo "the things of time are hidden from the blind." Ultimately, for Pozzo, man's existence is discomforting and futile, depressing, and gloomy and, most of all, brief and to no purpose. The gravedigger is the midwife of mankind: "They give birth astride the grave, the light gleams an instant, then it's night once more."

Lucky

As noted above, Lucky is the obvious antithesis of Pozzo. At one point, Pozzo maintains that Lucky's entire existence is based upon pleasing him; that is, Lucky's enslavement is his meaning, and if he is ever freed, his life would cease to have any significance. Given Lucky's state of existence, his very name "Lucky" is ironic, especially since Vladimir observes that even "old dogs have more dignity."

All of Lucky's actions seem unpredictable. In Act I, when Estragon attempts to help him, Lucky becomes violent and kicks him on the leg. When he is later expected to dance, his movements are as ungraceful and alien to the concept of dance as one can possibly conceive. We have seldom encountered such ignorance; consequently, when he is expected to give a coherent speech, we are still surprised by his almost total incoherence. Lucky seems to be more animal than human, and his very existence in the drama is a parody of human existence. In Act II, when he arrives completely dumb, it is only a fitting extension of his condition in Act I, where his speech was virtually incomprehensible. Now he makes no attempt to utter any sound at all. Whatever part of man that Lucky represents, we can make the general observation that he, as man, is reduced to leading the blind, not by intellect, but by blind instinct.

Endgame

"Nothing to be done" are the opening words of *Waiting for Godot*, and the line characterizes the entire drama. Likewise, the opening words of *Endgame*: "Finished, it's finished . . ." set the theme for this drama. These are the last words that Christ murmured on the cross: "It is finished." It is the end of the game. Beckett himself once described *Endgame* as being "rather difficult and elliptic" and as "more inhuman than *Godot*."

Part of the difficulty of the play lies in the condensation of the language. *Act Without Words I*, of course, has no language in it, but in *Endgame*, Beckett reduces language to its smallest denominator. It is even difficult for many to glean even the barest essentials of the drama. First, we cannot even be certain as to the nature of the setting itself. On the stage, we see a rather sparse, dim room with two small, high windows, one that looks out on land and the other on sea. There are two "ashbins" (ash cans) and a large object covered with a sheet. At first, the ash cans are also covered with a sheet, and thus the opening setting resembles a furniture storage house without any sign of life. The setting alone suggests various approaches to the play. The characters are confined to this bare room, which could suggest such diverse things as the inside of the human skull with the windows being the eyes to look out onto the world, or as one critic has suggested, we are within the womb. Outside the room, there is only devastation, with no sign of life (except maybe a small boy, if he exists, who (perhaps) appears towards the end of the play). The setting, therefore, is typical of Beckett; it is bizarre and unfamiliar, one that can evoke multiple associations and interpretations.

Against this decaying setting, the action (or non-action) of the drama is enacted, and it begins as it ends, with the words "it is finished," and the rest of the play deals with the end of the game. Unlike traditional drama, *Endgame* has no beginning and no middle; it opens at the end of a chess game, or at the end of life, or at the end of the world, and there is only "the impossible heap" that is left outside. In addition to the biblical echoes of Christ's last words, there are also various allusions throughout the play to the Christian story and to other biblical parallels. There are also Shakespearean allusions, along with multilingual puns and various, strategic chess moves. (For example, at the end of a chess game, only a few pieces remain on the board. Clov, with his cloven feet, hops about the stage as does the chess knight (or horse), and he is seen moving the "king" (Hamm) about the board one square at a time, but essentially he allows the king to remain stationary (whenever possible). Consequently, among the difficulties of the play are the non-action and the language, which has been reduced to a virtual non-language, but which is nevertheless filled with allusions to a great body of diverse literature.

At the opening, Hamm, who is blind, and Clov, who cannot sit, speak disjointedly about their life together; they are bored with one another and have lived together too long, but Clov can't leave because there is "nowhere else," and he can't kill Hamm because "I don't know the combination of the cupboard." Hamm controls what food or sustenance there is—thereby forcing the others to be subservient to his wishes. After Hamm inquires about his pain-killer and asks some seemingly irrelevant questions about some nonexistent bicycle wheels, Clov departs; the lid on one of the ash cans lifts, and Nagg, Hamm's father, looks out and asks for food. We hear that Nagg has no legs, only stumps, and is always kept in one of the ash cans. Clov returns, gives Nagg a biscuit, and as Nagg begins to nag about the biscuit, Clov forces him back into the ash can and closes the lid. After a brief discussion about Clov's seeds, which "haven't sprouted" (an allusion to Eliot's *Wasteland*), Clov departs.

Nagg reappears in his ash can and knocks on the adjacent ash can. Nell, Nagg's wife and Hamm's mother, appears and they reminisce about how they lost their legs in an accident on a tandem bicycle in northern France. Then they remember another incident which happened long ago, when they were engaged and were rowing on Lake Como. Then, Nagg told a story about a tailor who took longer to make a pair of striped trousers than it took God to make the world. But, according to the tailor, the trousers were better made than is the world. Hamm then whistles for Clov, who returns, and Nagg and Nell are forced back into their ash cans and the lids are replaced.

After Clov takes Hamm for a spin about the room and returns him to the exact center of the room, Hamm wants Clov to look out a window and report to him. Clov must get the stepladder (he has either shrunk or else the windows have risen) and the telescope. He looks out and reports that there is "Zero . . . (*He looks*) . . . zero . . . (*He looks*) . . . and zero."

After a discussion about the state of the earth (they wonder what would happen if a rational being came back to the earth), Clov discovers a flea on himself, which occupies his complete attention. Afterwards, Hamm wants to get on a raft and go somewhere, and he reminds Clov that someday Clov will be "like me. You'll be sitting there, a speck in the void, in the dark, forever." (The blind Pozzo in *Waiting for Godot* also says approximately the same thing: "One day I went blind, one day we'll go deaf . . . one day we shall die . . . is that not enough . . . .") Hamm then promises to give Clov the combination to the cupboard if Clov will promise "to finish me." When Clov refuses, Hamm reminds Clov of the time long ago when Clov first came here and Hamm was "a father" to him. This thought causes Hamm to ask for his toy dog to play with.

Suddenly, Hamm asks about Mother Pegg and if her light is on and whether or not she is buried, but Clov replies that he has had nothing to do with her or her burial. Then Hamm wants his "gaff," or stick, to move the chair; also, he wants the wheels (casters) oiled, but they were oiled yesterday, and yesterday was like all other days —"All life long the same inanities." Hamm wants to tell his story, but when Clov refuses to listen to it, Hamm insists that he awaken Nagg to listen to the story.

Hamm's story involves a man who comes crawling towards him on his belly. The man wants "bread for his brat." Hamm has no bread, but maybe there is a pot of porridge. The man asks Hamm to take in his child—if the child is still alive. Hamm can still see the man, "his hands flat on the ground, glaring . . . with his mad eyes." The story will soon be finished unless Hamm decides to "bring in other characters."

Hamm whistles for Clov, who excitedly exclaims that he's found a rat in the kitchen. Despite the fact that Clov has only extermi-nated "half the rat," Hamm says that can wait; for the present, they must all "pray to God." After several futile attempts to pray, Hamm concludes: "The bastard! He doesn't exist."

When Hamm's father begins wailing for a sugar plum, he reminds his son of how he used to cry in the night. Nagg and Nell let him cry, even moved him "out of earshot" so they could sleep in peace. Someday, Nagg warns, Hamm will cry out again for his father. He then sinks back into his ash can and closes the lid behind him.

Clov begins to straighten up the room ("I love order"), and he wonders how Hamm is progressing with his story (his chronicle). Hamm says that he has made some progress with the story—up to the point where the man wants to bring a small child with him to tend Hamm's garden, but the creative effort has exhausted him.

Hamm then inquires about his parents. Clov looks into the ash cans and reports that it looks as though Nell is dead, but Nagg is not; Nagg is crying. Hamm's only reaction is to ask to be moved by the window where he wants to hear the sea, but Clov tells him that this is impossible. After he checks on Nagg once again, refusing to kiss Hamm or even to give a hand to hold, Clov exits to check on the trapped rat in the kitchen.

Alone, Hamm ruminates almost incoherently about life and possible death and then blows his whistle for Clov; he inquires whether or not the rat got away and about his pain-killer. It is finally time for it, he says, but now "there is no more pain-killer." Hamm then wants Clov to look through the windows and give him a report. Clov looks out "at this muckheap," but it is not clear enough to see anything. Hamm wonders "what happened." For Clov, whatever happened doesn't matter, and he reminds Hamm that when Hamm refused to give old Mother Pegg some oil for her lamps, he knew that she would die "of boredom."

Clov, when ordered to get something, wonders why he always obeys Hamm, and Hamm suggests that perhaps it's because of compassion. As Clov is about to look out through the telescope, Hamm demands his toy dog. When Clov throws it to him, Hamm tells Clov to hit him with an axe or with his stick, but not with the dog. He would like to be placed in his coffin, but "there are no more coffins." Clov looks out the window toward "the filth" and says that it will be the last time; this is to be the end of the game. Suddenly, he sees something that "looks like a small boy." Clov wants to go see, but Hamm is against it. Hamm then announces that "it's the end, Clov; we've come to the end." Hamm says he doesn't need Clov anymore, and Clov prepares to leave. He makes a final speech to Hamm: "You must learn to suffer better . . . if you want them to weary of punishing you." Clov then exits while Hamm asks one last favor, but Clov doesn't hear it. In a few moments, Clov reenters, dressed for traveling. He stands impassively while Hamm continues his chronicle about the man coming to him, wanting to bring a child. At the end, Hamm calls out to Nagg and then to Clov. With no answer, he then covers his face with his handkerchief as the curtain falls.

One could easily conclude from the above that nothing happens, and this is part of Beckett's purpose. The world ends, according to T. S. Eliot, not with a bang but with a whimper. In this play, most of the things that Western civilization has stood for seem no longer to matter—God, family ties, respect for parents, love, prayer, loyalty, and religion—everything is meaningless here as the end of the game is being played; everything outside is *zero*. The only people remaining are sterile and despairing (one rotting); they "have had enough of this thing."

In *Endgame,* as in so many of his other plays, Beckett utilizes several sets of polarities which characterize most of his plays (*Act Without Words I* is something of an exception to the rule). Among the most obvious polarities here are (1) Hamm versus Clov: Hamm, when he is uncovered, is seen immediately to be a mass of decaying flesh in contrast to Clov, whose name is the same of a preservative spice—thus (2) decay versus preservative; (3) standing versus sitting: Clov must constantly move about the stage to preserve the status quo of the situation, giving us the polarity of (4) movement (Clov) versus non-movement (Hamm); (5) sight versus blindness: not only is Hamm decaying, but he is also blind and must rely upon Clov to see all things for him. The (6) master versus slave polarity is similar to the Pozzo-Lucky polarity; Pozzo and Hamm as masters are blind and must be led (or attended to) by the slaves, Lucky and Clov; (7) inside versus outside polarities are emphasized by the (8) left and right windows, through which Clov is able to report what is going on outside; (9) Nagg and Nell, the parents of Hamm, seem to suggest the muckheap which Beckett sees mankind as being. Ultimately, the concept (10) of life versus death informs most of the play. Whereas twice in *Waiting for Godot,* Vladimir and Estragon consider suicide by hanging, the idea of death pervades this entire play, from its title (the End of the Game) to the presumed death of Nell during the play and includes death images throughout the play —all indicating the possible death and fall of civilization as we know it. These, at least, are part of the complex polarities and images which Beckett uses in investigating man's absurd existence in an absurd world.

All That Fall

Unlike Beckett's other works, *All That Fall* was commissioned by the British Broadcasting Corporation (BBC) explicitly for radio presentation. This work can be considered as a type of contrasting companion piece to *Act Without Words I,* a play that has no dialogue, no spoken words, and no sound effects except the sound of a whistle; the play relies entirely on mime. In contrast, *All That Fall* relies a great deal for its impact on sound effects and a very careful attention to the spoken word and the various death images that run throughout the play.

In outline form, the play could be said to most resemble the structure of *Don Quixote*—that is, it is picaresque; in the same way that the old, decrepit Don Quixote sallied forth and encountered a series of adventures, usually of an absurd nature, in *All That Fall*, Mrs. Maddy Rooney (in her seventies) is found to be on a difficult journey to the train station to meet her blind husband. On the way, she has a series of ludicrous or absurd adventures. First, she meets the local dung carrier, who tries to sell her a load of dung which she does not need. After he drags his "cleg-tormented" hinny (a sterile, hybrid animal resembling a mule) and dung wagon away, we hear the sound of a bicycle bell, and Mr. Tyler, a retired bill-broker squeaks to a stop. While telling how his daughter's operation rendered her barren, he is almost killed by a passing motor van, which covers them "white with dust from head to foot," making them interrupt their journey until "this vile dust falls back upon the viler worms." As the two travel onward, she bemoans the death of her only daughter, Minnie.

After Mr. Tyler pedals off on his bicycle, Mr. Slocum (slow come), a clerk of the racecourse, draws up beside her in his automobile and offers her a ride. She is, however, too old and fat to climb in alone, and Mr. Slocum has to push her in. He tries to start the car, but it has died. After finally getting it started again, he drives over a hen, killing her. Arriving at the station, the porter, Tommy, tries to help Mrs. Rooney down, but she is stuck. After great effort, Tommy and Mr. Slocum free her, and the latter drives away, "crucifying his gearbox."

The station master, Mr. Barrell, inquires about Mrs. Rooney's health and hears from her that she should still be in bed: "Would I were still in bed, Mr. Barrell. Would I were lying stretched out in my comfortable bed, Mr. Barrell, just wasting slowly, painlessly away. . . ." We then hear of the death of Mr. Barrell's father, a story which reminds Mrs. Rooney of many of her own sorrows. Miss Fitt is then seen approaching, but she is so absorbed in humming a hymn that she does not see Mrs. Rooney, who reminds her that they worshipped together the preceding Sunday. Miss Fitt, a misfit, asserts strongly that she does not notice things of this world, and she does not help Mrs. Rooney up the station stairs.

The train is late, an occurrence that has not happened within the memory of any of the characters. An explanation is demanded of the station master, Mr. Barrell: "Please a statement of some kind. . . . Even the slowest train on this brief line is not ten minutes and more behind its scheduled time without good cause." At last, the train arrives, and Mr. Rooney (Dan), who is blind, is helped from the train by a small boy, Jerry, whom they immediately dismiss with a small tip. The Rooneys carefully descend the steps and begin the arduous journey home. Mrs. Rooney then stops to inquire about the reason for the lateness of the train. Her husband refuses to discuss the subject, and they continue on their journey.

Suddenly they feel threatened by two children hiding and jeering at them. Mr. Rooney wonders if Mrs. Rooney has ever wished "to kill a child." He speaks of his desire to live at home, simply, with no cares or tribulations. On the way, he explains how he got on the train, how it started, and then stopped. Being blind, he could see no reason for it to stop unless it had reached a station, but this was not true. After some time, the train moved on and he arrived at his home station.

Mr. Rooney then requests, "Say something, Maddy. Say something." Mrs. Rooney, to pass time, tells about a specialist on "the troubled mind" who treated a "very strange and unhappy" little girl: "The only thing wrong with her as far as he could see was that she was dying. And she did, in fact, die, shortly after he washed his hands of her." Mrs. Rooney went to the specialist, she says, because of her "lifelong preoccupation with horses' buttocks." Her concern was directly correlated with the sexual nature of the ass (or hinny) that Christ rode into Jerusalem.

In the distance, they hear faint strains of Shubert's "Death and the Maiden" song, which prompts Mr. Rooney to inquire about the text of Sunday's sermon: it is "The Lord upholdeth all that fall and raiseth up all those that be bowed down."

Jerry suddenly catches up with them in order to return something that Mr. Rooney dropped; as Jerry is about to leave, Mrs. Rooney asks about "the hitch . . . what kept the train so late." Jerry explains that it was "because a little child fell out of the carriage, Ma'am. On the line, Ma'am. Under the wheels, Ma'am."

As the action denotes, the most commonplace events are constantly surrounded by death or signs, symbols, and reminders of death. The absurdity of the play lies partly in the comic, grotesque nature of Mrs. Rooney and the other characters in the drama. But even in the most grotesque, there is something of the commonplace and even in the most common and vulgar, there is an element that transcends the ordinary. Mrs. Rooney's speech, which is ordinary and common, is sprinkled with unusual expressions and bizarre syntax. Early in the play, she tells Christy to "climb up on the crest of your manure and let yourself be carried along." Later in the play, Mr. Rooney comments on Mrs. Rooney's speech:

MR. ROONEY: I speak—and you listen to the wind.

MRS. ROONEY: No no, I am agog, tell me all, we shall press on and never pause, never pause till we come safe to haven.

MR. ROONEY: Never pause . . . safe to haven. . . . Do you know, Maddy, sometimes one would think you were struggling with a dead language.

Likewise, there are not many things more commonplace than the fact that a chicken is often run over and killed by a car on a country road. Yet, Mrs. Rooney's language becomes a literary eulogy in praise of the dead chicken:

What a death! One minute picking happy at the dung, on the road, in the sun, with now and then a dust bath, and then— bang!—all her troubles over. [*Pause.*] All the laying and the hatching. [*Pause.*] Just one great squawk and then . . . peace. [*Pause.*] They would have slit her weasand in any case. [*Pause.*]

Thus, we have on the one hand, the most common and elemental figures—characters one would find in any low comedy—yet on the other hand, these same characters are in constant confrontation with death. Images of a barren, sterile, and death-like world are constantly evoked. The uniqueness of the characters is that they continue to exist or endure (as did Vladimir and Estragon in *Waiting for Godot*) in an absurd world such as theirs, and the absurdity is emphasized by the juxtaposition of their ignorant commonplace natures in a world where death is indeed the most commonplace occurrence.

Among the images of barrenness, sterility, or death which are either evoked or used thematically are some of the following:

1. "Death and the Maiden" is the Schubert song which opens and closes the drama, thereby setting a death tone which is carried throughout.

2. Since this is a radio drama, various other sounds are constantly evoked, only to die slowly away.

3. In the first scene, Mrs. Rooney encounters the dung carrier, Christy, whose animal is a hinny, a hybrid between a horse and an ass, which is sterile; being unable to procreate, it dies with itself.

4. The encounter with the sterile hinny reminds Mrs. Rooney that her daughter, Minnie, also died barren, and there is no issue from her to survive.

5. Mr. Tyler arrives, and we hear that his daughter is barren and, therefore, he will always be grandchildless.

6. The flat tire on Mr. Tyler's bicycle becomes significant in the barrenness of the world around him.

7. Mrs. Rooney meets Mr. Slocum (slow come) and hears that his mother is dying and is usually in great pain.

8. Mr. Slocum's car dies, and he can get it started again only with difficulty.

9. Then Mr. Slocum runs over and kills the hen, allowing Mrs. Rooney to deliver her eulogy on the dead hen, an ode that is a parody on grandiose literary rhetoric.

10. Arriving at the station, Mrs. Rooney describes her condition in such a way as to evoke the image of a corpse being shrouded for burial: "Would I were lying stretched out in my comfortable bed. . . . "

11. Mrs. Rooney then hears about the death of Mr. Barrell's father, who died only a short time after receiving the job of station master.

12. Miss Fitt, a misfit in this world, believes herself to belong to a heavenly world and "left to myself would soon be flown home."

13. While Miss Fitt is helping Mrs. Rooney up the stairs, she begins to hum John Henry Newman's hymn "Lead, Kindly Light," which was sung on the *Titanic* as it was sinking.

14. Suddenly a female voice warns young Dolly not to stand close because "one can be sucked under." This, of course, anticipates the death of the young maiden at the end of the drama.

15. Mr. Tyler thinks that Miss Fitt has lost her mother, but it turns out that Miss Fitt simply cannot find her because the mother was to arrive on the last train, and Miss Fitt does not yet know that the last train has been detained; thus, since the mother is bringing fresh sole (soul), there is still hope that the mother is not lost.

16. Mr. Rooney (Dan) arrives, and he is blind and suffers from an old wound and a coronary.

17. Going home, the old man inquires of his old wife if she has ever had the desire to kill a child.

18. Mr. Rooney even sees the two of them in terms of Dante's great lovers, Paolo and Francesca, who were doomed to hell for adultery and were constantly locked in each other's arms. Thus, Mr. Rooney, who is blind, is locked to Mrs. Rooney, who is so decrepit that she can hardly move, an ironic reversal of the great lovers of Dante's *Inferno,* but the evocation reminds one of the sterility of the entire *Inferno.*

19. Mr. Rooney, in commenting on his wife's strange speech, thinks sometimes that she is "struggling with a dead language." Mrs. Rooney agrees, believing that her language will "be dead in time, just like our poor dear Gaelic" language is already dead.

20. Mrs. Rooney remembers a time when she went to a lecture about a cure for her "preoccupation with horses' buttocks," but she heard at the lecture, instead, a story about a young girl who had only one thing wrong with her—"the only thing wrong with her . . . was that she was dying." This then anticipates the death of the young maiden under the wheels of the train at the end of the drama.

21. As the drama nears its close, many death images converge —the leaves falling and rotting, the dead dog rotting in the ditch, the concern over whether Jesus rode a sterile hinny into Jerusalem, the wind and the rain, and the recurrence of the Schubert song "Death and the Maiden."

22. The text of the sermon thus furnishes the title for this drama: "The Lord upholdeth *all that fall.*" This is immedi-

ately followed by the reason for the train's being late: "It was a little child fell out of the carriage, Ma'am . . . on the line, Ma'am . . . under the wheels, Ma'am."

The above list contains some of the more prominent concerns with death or death-like images in the drama. From the comic eulogy on the dead hen to the horror of the innocent child being killed under the wheels of the train, the entire drama abounds in orchestration on the theme of death—some ludicrous and some filled with solemnity. The various sounds of the play contribute to the eerie effects and also remind us that among the familiar sounds, death is as commonplace as a hen crossing the road.

Act Without Words I

Whereas the characters in Beckett's plays usually exist in terms of pairs, *Act Without Words I* has a single figure upon an alien, desert landscape. This setting aligns it with *Waiting for Godot*, which also has a barren landscape and a single barren tree. In *Act Without Words I*, among the things that descend on the stage is a single tree with "a single bough some three yards from the ground and at its summit a meager tuft of palms." Against a barren desert landscape with "dazzling light," a single individual, "The Man," is thrown backwards upon the stage. The rest of the drama simply shows the actions (or the *acts*) of the man without any word spoken. There is, of course, the sense of another presence (another distant Godot or God) which is controlling "The Man's" actions, but we are never made aware of the nature of this other presence.

Act Without Words I can be seen as a contrasting piece to *All That Fall* in terms of pure dramatic technique. *All That Fall* relies totally upon voice and sound effects for its meaning and, in contrast, *Act Without Words I* is purely visual. It has no spoken word nor any sound effects, except the sound of a whistle. Some critics have debated whether or not *Act Without Words I* should be considered as drama. In traditional terms, it should not be, but it is definitely a work of the Theater of the Absurd. For example, since so many plays in this tradition have emphasized the failure of communication, Beckett has simply gone a step further and has written a play in which there is no dialogue whatsoever, yet this is a play in which significant intellectual concerns are suggested by the actions we observe.

The play opens with "The Man" being thrown *backwards* onto the stage. This action is repeated two more times to the accompaniment of a whistle and then later is repeated some more, for a total of four times. There is no visible sign of confinement; nor is there any indication that "The Man" is being flung backwards by a person, yet he is not allowed to leave the stage. Then other things begin to appear: a tree and a carafe of water. He can't reach the carafe, and some cubes begin to appear. After attempting to reach the carafe of water by stacking the cubes, only to have the cubes pulled from under him and the carafe moved beyond his reach, he then takes a rope which has descended, arranges one of the cubes next to the tree, and makes plans for suicide before he "hesitates, thinks better of it." Between each action, a whistle either directs his actions or calls attention to some aspect of the stage. Finally, "The Man" no longer hears the whistle, and he no longer responds to any outside stimuli. Like Vladimir and Estragon, who also reject suicide at the end of *Waiting for Godot* and are seen sitting perfectly motionless, so also is "The Man" inert at the end of *Act Without Words I*.

The most obvious intellectual analogy, of course, is to the ancient Greek myth of Tantalus, who was a mortal favored by the gods. The gods allowed Tantalus to dine with them on nectar and ambrosia, but he violated their trust by feeding these divine foods to his mortal friends. Later, he became so arrogant that he committed the ultimate atrocity: he killed his own son and served him to the gods, who recoiled in horror. For his sins, Tantalus was sentenced to eternal torment: he was placed in a pool of water, and whenever he tried to drink, the water receded. Above him were clusters of grapes (or fruit), and whenever he reached up, they receded. Thus, we have the English verb "to tantalize."

We must ask ourselves if "The Man" is being punished by some God, since, like Tantalus, each time he reaches for the carafe, it recedes. But unlike Tantalus, who seemingly continues throughout eternity to reach for the water and fruit, "The Man" abandons all efforts and at the end is content to lie on his side and stare at his hands, totally ignoring the whistle which earlier controlled his life. And unlike Tantalus who defied the gods, "The Man" does not defiantly shake his fist at God; he is content to stare at his hands and ignore all else. He might even be god-like, since the typical Deist depicts God as One sitting apart from the world with nothing to do but pare his fingernails. In addition, "The Man" is somewhat like God—silent and solitary.

As in *Waiting for Godot*, the use of the burlesque here undermines man's attempt to assert himself in an absurd world. The entire *Act Without Words I* could easily be part of any burlesque theater; it employs, as did *Waiting for Godot*, many of the Chaplinesque or burlesque techniques. "The Man" is flung backwards on the stage four different times, and each time he has the plucky courage of the little man who refuses to give up, who gets up from an undignified fall in order to confront again the opposing force. The comic element is there, despite the tragic emphasis on man's fallen state. The fact that the little man can do nothing about it is both laughable and pathetic, as was Chaplin. But neither the tragic element nor the comic element is allowed to dominate. A seat is pulled out from under "The Man," a rope which he climbs breaks, and again we realize that we are in the presence of the comic and the burlesque, yet "The Man" is pathetic and trapped. Thus Beckett's statement: man is comic and, at the same time, he is trapped and pathetic. Yet like Vladimir and Estragon, there is a sense of enduring; "The Man" ultimately refuses to play the game any longer; he refuses to respond or to reflect. He has silenced the whistle and is content with his inertia. Thus man's *act* without words is his *non-act* of doing absolutely nothing and saying absolutely nothing. In existential terms, a refusal to choose is a choice; here, "The Man's" refusal to *act* is in itself an *act*.

Krapp's Last Tape

Beckett was constantly experimenting with new forms of expression. After *All That Fall* (a radio drama largely dependent upon many sound effects) and *Act Without Words I,* he experimented further with a form often characterized as a "monodrama" and gave us the uniquely different *Krapp's Last Tape*. The title implies that Krapp, an old man who is hard of hearing and whose eyesight is failing, is making his last recorded tape soliloquy. (Some critics prefer to use the more vulgar suggestion that Krapp is crapping his last turd.) We later discover that through the years, he has been constantly recording observations about his life on tape; now, he sits in his rather sparsely furnished apartment listening to old tapes and making new ones. In fact, most of the play consists of listening to the voice of Krapp, recorded on a tape thirty years earlier. This is another dramatic *tour de force* in terms of structural concepts— that is, Krapp's present voice, taping a tape for the future, is juxtaposed against Krapp's past voice, recorded on a tape thirty years ago. And to make the situation even more complicated, the present voice is supposed to be set in the future, thus making the past voice actually in the present.

Like many other Beckett characters, Krapp belongs to the world of the outcasts. He is dressed in "rusty black" trousers and waistcoat with a dirty white shirt. He looks rather like one of the derelicts in Beckett's other plays. The emphasis on the white face and purple nose suggests that he is another of Beckett's "music hall" characters. Similar to the munching of turnips and carrots which Vladimir and Estragon eat in *Waiting for Godot*, here Krapp eats bananas during the scene and, from the voice on the tape, we know that he ate bananas thirty years earlier.

The tape which he chooses to listen to was recorded when he was thirty-nine years old, and as he moves the tape on fast forward, we hear in disjointed segments, references to the three bananas that he has just eaten, to his mother's dying after a long "viduity" (widowhood), to a dog, to a storm and darkness, and to various descriptions of the progress and dissolution of a love affair when "I lay down across her with my face in her breasts and my hand on her." Ultimately, the love affair dissolves, and its dissolution becomes central to the past tape.

In listening to the voice of the tape of the past and hearing Krapp's present voice utter the same longing (Krapp's present voice says: "All that old misery. Once wasn't enough. Lie down across her."), we realize that the passing of thirty years has been insignificant. Krapp is still troubled by this love affair, which he tried unsuccessfully to dismiss thirty years ago, but he still returns to listen again and again about its dissolution and failure.

The suggested failure of the love affair was a failure of communication. Krapp tries to discover his own identity in the image that he finds in the eyes of his beloved, but in staring into her eyes, he sees only a reflection of himself. His insistent plea—"let me in"—is not a sexual plea so much as it is a metaphysical plea to be accepted into her world. (The sexual imagery, especially that of their moving "up and down," and other movements is obvious, as is the pun upon Krapp's name, but the imagery throughout transcends the purely physical in the manner that John Donne's poetic sexual imagery is also metaphysical.) Since his romantic breakup, Krapp's world has been aligned to his mother's world, and both have existed in a "viduity" for years. Krapp's only communication now is with the spool of his last tape.·

Just as nothing changes in the lives of Vladimir and Estragon during *Waiting for Godot*, nothing has changed in the thirty years between Krapp's last tape and the present moment. He still eats bananas, he still voices the same concerns, he is still isolated from the world, and he is still plagued by his same hopes and despairs. As the tape ends, the voice of thirty years ago maintains that "My best years are gone. . . ." But the irony is that thirty years have passed and he is still playing the tape, still living in the same world, and as the curtain falls, "The tape runs on in silence." As we leave the theater, neither Krapp nor his tape is heard. Man can no longer communicate—even with himself.

SELECTED BIBLIOGRAPHY

CHEVIGNY, B. G. (ed.). *Twentieth Century Interpretations of Endgame: A Collection of Critical Essays*. Prentice-Hall, 1961.

COE. R. N. *Beckett*. Oliver and Boyd, 1964.

COHN, RUBY. *Beckett: The Comic Gamut*. Rutgers University Press, 1962

————. *(ed.). A Casebook on Waiting for Godot*. Grove Press, 1967.

ESSLIN, MARTIN. *The Theater of the Absurd*. London, 1968.

————. *Samuel Beckett: A Collection of Critical Essays*. Prentice-Hall, 1965.

HOFFMAN, FREDERICK J. *Samuel Beckett: The Language of Self*. New York, 1964.